The General's
Game Book

By the same author

Cordon and Search
(Gale & Polden, 1949)
Republished by Battery Press, USA, 1984
Republished as *With 6th Airborne Division in Palestine 1945-48* by Pen & Sword, 2008

Tempting the Fates
(Pen & Sword, 2006)

The General's Game Book

The Sporting Life of a Military Gentleman

Dare Wilson

Pen & Sword
MILITARY

First published in Great Britain in 2013 by
Pen & Sword Military
an imprint of
Pen & Sword Books Ltd
47 Church Street
Barnsley
South Yorkshire
S70 2AS

Copyright © Dare Wilson 2013

ISBN 978 1 78303 005 7

The right of Dare Wilson to be identified as the Author of this Work
has been asserted by him in accordance with the Copyright, Designs
and Patents Act 1988.

A CIP catalogue record for this book is available from the British
Library

Typeset in Ehrhardt by
Mac Style, Driffield, East Yorkshire
Printed and bound in the UK by CPI Group (UK) Ltd, Croydon,
CRO 4YY

Pen & Sword Books Ltd incorporates the Imprints of Pen & Sword
Aviation, Pen & Sword Maritime, Pen & Sword Military, Wharncliffe
Local History, Pen and Sword Select, Pen & Sword Military Classics,
Leo Cooper, The Praetorian Press, Remember When, Seaforth
Publishing and Frontline Publishing.

For a complete list of Pen & Sword titles please contact
PEN & SWORD BOOKS LIMITED
47 Church Street, Barnsley, South Yorkshire, S70 2AS, England
E-mail: enquiries@pen-and-sword.co.uk
Website: www.pen-and-sword.co.uk

Contents

Acknowledgements

My thanks are many and various: to the St Moritz Tobogganing Club for permission to reproduce two items that originally appeared in an Annual Report; to Dominic Berridge for updating me on the Wexford Slobs; to the friends whose reminiscences have stimulated my own memories; to Henry Wilson of Pen & Sword for his encouragement to write this book; and to my wife for having the patience to live with an author as well as typing every word I have written and providing valuable comments.

To Sarah,
again

And in memory of my father Sydney, who taught me to shoot and was still himself shooting creditably at the age of 90, my mother Dorothea, who taught all her four children to ride and herself rode to hounds for 80 years, and my Labrador Dinah, who almost certainly saved my life during the historic blizzard of 1942.

Chapter 1

The Seeds are Sown

Before the Industrial Revolution, and the demand for coal that it stimulated, the counties of Durham and Northumberland must have been among the most beautiful in England. Many parts of them still are beautiful, but when coal from the North East became famous for its quality, collieries multiplied, with an inevitable impact on the landscape. The ugly silhouettes of pit winding gear and slagheaps appeared, and the railway spread its network. All this was accepted as the price of employment and wealth, but much of the landscape remained unspoiled. Rivers, the lower reaches of which passed through the industrial areas, were often unblemished higher up, and secluded valleys winding through ancient broadleaved woodlands opened on to moorland of breathtaking beauty. Such a valley was that of the Northumbrian River Derwent, the principal tributary of the Tyne, itself once the premier salmon river of England and now, in the twenty-first century, proudly holding that position again in landscape no longer despoiled with slagheaps, though threatened with ever increasing urban development.

There, close to the county boundary of Durham and Northumberland, I was born in 1919 in Priestfield Lodge, a large house between Burnopfield and Shotley Bridge. The life I enjoyed was very different from that of later generations, and I am constantly reminded how much times have changed. In my own case, when recalling my boyhood, I am conscious of the freedom, then taken for granted, of those born immediately following one world war and brought up before the next. Few of today's problems restricting the liberty of children to enjoy a wholesome degree of independence existed then, and many of us who were brought up in country surroundings were not only permitted but positively encouraged by our parents to explore woodlands and remote areas, to discover for ourselves what we might in our rapidly widening world.

As well as the freedom to roam independently there were organized pursuits. My mother was well known for her affinity with horses and took it for granted that every healthy child, given the opportunity, would wish to ride a pony and, as soon as possible, follow hounds. She herself hunted for eighty years, having begun with her father in Yorkshire at the age of six, continued in Durham and Northumberland and finally enjoyed the sport on Exmoor, reluctantly pensioning off her hunter when she was eighty-six. As children we were never asked if or when we would like to hunt; it was assumed our enthusiasm for it was as strong as her own. When hounds met within reach of home on a cub-hunting morning, family reveille at 4.30 am was the norm. An equilibrium was only established in my case through my father who, though a good horseman, was keener on shooting and, later in life, fishing, pursuits which eventually assumed pride of place in my own interests.

However, at the age of six I was too young to shoot and too impatient to fish, so I was taken hunting with the Braes of Derwent Foxhounds, a private pack owned by Lewis Priestman of Shotley Bridge, who was Master for forty-nine years. My mount was Mousie, a Shetland pony who had previously carried my two elder sisters, Kitty and Betty, and would eventually carry my younger brother Peter; altogether, four generations of our family hunted with the Braes. While I was still relatively new to hunting Mother stopped insisting on having me always by her side, and Mousie and I were given our freedom. Mousie was a character, sometimes with ideas of his own; but we soon reached a more or less workable understanding that, provided neither of us was too difficult, we would each overlook the other's shortcomings. So I continued to spit my raisin pips between Mousie's ears and he would still suggest it was time to go home long before I considered that necessary.

When an appropriate occasion arose at the end of a hunt, I was informed that the huntsman, Alfred Littleworth, had suggested the time had come for me to be 'blooded'. For those who are unfamiliar with these niceties, this amounted to having one's cheeks wiped with some part of the dead fox, leaving a smear of warm blood. As he was performing this rite Alfred warned me that at bedtime someone might wish to wash it off, but this, in his view, was quite unnecessary. I was duly prepared, and when Nanny began to clean me in the bath I quoted Alfred. Nanny and I were both adamant, and a storm of unprecedented ferocity ensued before Mother had to be fetched. Unfortunately, Alfred and I lost the battle.

Before I was eight years old I began fishing in the River Derwent above Shotley Bridge, where brown trout were plentiful, and, following the accepted practice of those days, I started with a worm. I was put in the care of Geordie Hall, a retired keeper and a great character who taught me much country lore as well as fishing. Initially I used my mother's old greenheart rod, but before long I bought my very own fly rod, handmade of split cane and costing me thirty shillings (£1.50), from W.R. Pape of Newcastle. As a junior member of the Derwent Angling Association I paid an annual subscription of two shillings and sixpence (12½p). For this I could fish some twenty miles of the river, the upper reaches of which were remarkably beautiful. Often I fished them through a long day without meeting another soul, and rarely did I return home with an empty creel. The Association was part of the Northumbrian Anglers Federation, the president of which at the time was Viscount Grey of Falloden, himself a keen fisherman. I still treasure my copy of the Federation's Handbook and Guide dated 1930. The members were a splendid cross section of fishermen from all walks of life, not a few of whom were coal miners. One day, as I was playing a good trout, one of them watched me manoeuvre it into my net before expressing his approval.

A most remarkable piece of good fortune came in my early teens, when a generous friend of my father's learned that I was keen on fishing. He had the lease of a prime stretch of the River Coquet and, being preoccupied with his business, was rarely able to enjoy it himself. Having no family of his own, he invited me to go whenever I wished, telling me just to mention it first to Oliver, the gamekeeper, who watched the river and would keep an eye on me. My journeys to the Coquet involved catching two buses, one into Newcastle and then another northwards for an hour to Felton. Depending on my age, my parents set limits for the time I had to return home, knowing that the buses ran at intervals through the day and night, mainly for coal miners going on and off shift. On one occasion I had had a particularly successful day, catching all the fish I could carry. My creel was so full the lid would not fasten and, although I did my best to tie it down, it was not secure. Because I was late for the bus I was hurrying along the path beside a mill race, with a steady flow of water running down the leat. I then had to cross a wooden bridge and while doing so slipped on the wet timber. My creel slid round and its insecure lid flew open. My entire catch of fish cascaded on to the bridge and then slithered into the leat below. I watched as they drifted into the slow current and eventually sank into its deeper sections, still just visible from the bridge. I was distraught at the loss of the best catch of my young life and, with the imminent departure of the bus no longer in mind, resolved to follow the leat down to the mill and explain to the miller what had befallen me, though I did not seriously think he could assist, as the mill was in full operation grinding corn at the time.

The miller was a friendly Northumbrian and listened patiently to my tale of woe. "Well," he exclaimed at the end of my account. "What do you expect me to do?" I explained that I wished to climb down into the leat and see what I could retrieve from the flowing water, but had thought I should first seek his permission. When he learned what my hard-earned catch meant to me he asked how long it would take me if he stopped the mill. When I replied that I could do it in just a few minutes he said, "Right, hurry back and I'll have the mill stopped by the time you get there." He was as good as his word and I recovered every fish. Today, more then eighty years on, he remains in my memory as a person who did me an exceptionally good turn.

That was during the most prolonged period of the finest fishing I ever enjoyed. Those were the days before water abstraction had affected the flow, and the Coquet was in every sense still a noble river, teeming with salmon and sea trout as well as brown trout. I continued to enjoy the privilege of fishing it through the 1930s, during the war when I was home on leave, and thereafter until 1949 when my parents moved south. It was on that river, as a boy, that I lost the leviathan of my life, a fish which appeared to exceed in size any salmon I had seen before. Although by the time this happened I was equipped to handle a large fish, this one took charge from the start and, without pause, covered the length of the Quarry Stream and a long stretch below, with me following and still in distant contact, until it disappeared over Felton dam. Then the line went slack, and the sense of disappointment was overwhelming. It was also on the River Coquet as a boy that I learned to fish for sea trout at night, eventually, and ever since, with a trio of flies. More often than not the best sport was on the darkest nights, and I sometimes took a break in the small hours to doze on the river bank, before resuming the challenge posed by that incomparable species shortly before dawn.

I believe it is during boyhood that the seeds are sown which grow into the natural countryman. By that I mean someone with highly developed senses who is at ease in all situations in remote areas, particularly at night. This confidence and feeling of wellbeing when alone in the dark, far from roads and habitation, is in my experience only found in a minority of people, and those I have known have all been brought up in the country. Many years later, when in my military career I became responsible for training young soldiers how to move silently by night, I learned how many grown men brought up in an illuminated urban environment are afraid of being alone in remote countryside on dark nights.

For my eighth birthday I was given a .410 shotgun. My father, who was a very experienced shot, gave me a thorough grounding in the essentials of safety and etiquette and made it quite clear that I was never to take the gun out alone until, in due course, I received permission to do so. 'Normal procedure', some might murmur to themselves, and so it should be. But little did either of us realize how soon such an occasion would arise. In September 1927, a month after my birthday, I was sent to Harecroft Hall, a boarding preparatory school in the Lake District. It was without doubt a remarkable school, in some ways epitomising the concept of Outward Bound training before Kurt Hahn founded Gordonstoun. The headmaster was R.A. Vallance, a middle-aged veteran of the First World War, who believed that the primary responsibility of a private school should be to develop character and manners. The school prospectus contained twenty-three photographs of boys engaged in school activities. Ten showed ponies, then there were three of boys haymaking (with ponies), two of boys mowing the lawn (one with the assistance of a pony), one of boys fishing, four of sports teams and three of expeditions to the Lakes. It was left to the reader to assume that somewhere indoors there might be form rooms, dormitories and other conventionally desirable facilities.

Some afternoons at Harecroft were set aside for supervised games, but on others we were allowed to find our own amusements. There was a stream where we sailed our toy boats, and we also helped to keep the spacious grounds tidy. I still have a scar on the bridge of my nose where an overenthusiastic friend standing next in line caught me with his shovel as we were digging out what was to become the swimming pool. One day, when seeking permission to explore further afield than usual, I noticed what I thought was a .410 shotgun in the headmaster's study. When I commented on it I was questioned closely about my experience with firearms, and to my surprise and delight was then asked if I would like to take it out in the school grounds late one afternoon to shoot starlings, which had taken to roosting there in such large numbers that they were fouling the ground beneath the trees. I was given several cartridges and instructed to give an account of how I used each one when I returned the gun. Such was the density of roosting birds that I was able to get several with one shot, and soon my total exceeded the number of cartridges fired. On giving my report it seemed that I had passed my first test.

In due course Mr Vallance extended his permission to include rabbits on the school farm, and I thoroughly enjoyed stalking and shooting them. One day while I was doing this a small covey of partridges rose in front of me, and without pausing to consider if I was permitted to shoot at them I did so. I brought one back to the headmaster's study, by then wondering if I had broken the rules, but I need not have worried. "Well done", he said quietly. "Next time, make it a right and left." A few days later, on 3 February 1930, I wrote a letter on school headed paper to my father; many years later he returned it to me to insert in my first game book, where it has remained:

Dear Daddy,
    Many happy returns of the day. I hope you will have a very happy birthday.
    Last Wednesday I shot 1 partridge flying, it fell 25 yards from me.
    And I am going to have it for dinner to day with another boy. I did the same as you!
    Its wate was 13 oz.
      With lots of love
        from
          Dare
    P.S. (afterdinner). I had It for dinner, just now with another boy it was
                joly good."

In planning all forms of work and activity the headmaster was more interested in the boys' approach and outlook than in mere achievement. The ethos of his system was that the key to success, whether in learning or other fields, lay largely in character training. This, in his view, enabled children to recognize obligations and priorities and, above all, where duty lies. This, he maintained, strengthened the mental and physical capacity to resist fear and temptation. Thus character becomes the dominant force in personal performance and in the contribution of the individual within a collective enterprise. As an example of how Mr Vallance applied his concept, I vividly recall one winter night before I was halfway up the school, when he invited me to accompany him alone on a rat-hunt in the stables, which were at that time infested with the pests. The plan was that he would enter the stables, whereupon the rats would bolt through the drainpipe into the stable yard. Here I would stand, holding a sack across the open pipe to catch the bolting animals. Having not done it or even seen it done before, the idea did not appeal to me, but one did not admit such feelings to the headmaster. I held the sack as instructed, and out they came one after another until the sack heaved with squealing rodents. In due course, after he had completed a circuit of the stables banging on the bins and bedding, Mr Vallance reappeared and, taking the sack from me, swung it round his head and against the wall several times before tipping out the dead contents. He then thanked me casually, as though he had never doubted my readiness to assist. I naturally did my best to leave him with the impression that my first name was 'Ratcatcher' and that I had enjoyed every moment.

At home I was particularly fond of my mother's father, George Burgess, who lived nearby. He was a lovely old man with a rich sense of humour, a great love of music and a fine bass voice, but it was his prowess as a horseman for which he was best known, in an age when riding was commonplace and driving a team of horses was still much admired. He had a way with horses that was fascinating and most in evidence when he was driving a coach and four. Somehow his team seemed to sense what was expected of them and responded in a way that old hands in the art of driving recognized as showing a master's touch. At some stage he had befriended Lewis Priestman, who was not only master and owner of the Braes of Derwent Foxhounds but also owner of the 'Venture' coach, which followed a scheduled run until the outbreak of the Second World War. According to *The Field* in 1943:

The present war ended the run of three hundred years of coaching on English roads. The famous 'Venture' coach, the last of the regular stage coaches, ceased to run in 1939. From 1924 every summer it ran three days per week, through some of the finest country-side of Northumberland and Durham. The yellow and scarlet panelled coach, with its team of greys, was driven by its owner, Mr Lewis Priestman, of Shotley Bridge. Will Payne, with scarlet coat and beaver topper, the famous guard, played the coach horn. In these modern days it was a sight never to be forgotten, a reminder of those long-vanished times when the roads of England were the high-ways of adventure and romance.

Not infrequently Lewis Priestman required a relief driver and called on Grandfather to assist. He never lost the art and would drive his team at a smart trot over Derwent Bridge, with its near right-angled turns at either end. There were two teams of four greys, one for the outward run to Edmondbyers, where a tea was served of which Jorrocks would have approved, and one for the return to Shotley Bridge. In addition there were two 'cockhorses' waiting at the bottom of the steeper stretches, increasing each team to six. The changes were effected by the grooms with a dexterity that would have done justice to the Royal Tournament.

During the mid-1930s I was a keen blower of brazen instruments at school, and this led to the conferment on me of Grandfather's treasured 46" coach horn, bearing his name and an inscription, given to him by a group of friends in 1883, which I was taught to play by Will Payne. I learned all the old coaching calls from *Ye Coachhorn Tootles*, published by Boosey & Hawkes, and from other even more ancient manuals, and it was not long before I was invited to join Will Payne on the back of the coach. There I met the problem of blowing the horn on a swaying deck and had to learn to stand with knees slightly bent to act as shock-absorbers. There was something very romantic about delivering a melodic old coaching tune to the rolling countryside on a fine summer afternoon, when it would carry across the valley far enough to reach the distant farms. So it happened that, without realizing it, I blew the horn on the 'Venture' on what proved to be its last scheduled run at the end of August 1939.

Chapter 2

Problems on the Wash

During school holidays, on appropriate occasions, my father took me to grouse moors and pheasant shoots that he shared with the small group of friends with whom he had shot over many years. There I watched how the days were organized and helped to pick up and carry game. After a few years, when I had settled into the routine, I was invited to bring my gun and initially was always placed on a flank, with my father next to me in the line.

But however much I enjoyed game shooting there was another aspect of the sport which would influence my priorities in the future, and that was wildfowling. My introduction to this was indirectly linked with my mother's commitment to the Pony Club, and in particular the assistance she gave to a promising young member named Nancy Angus, who became an accomplished horsewoman. In return for my mother's encouragement Nancy asked if I might be interested in being taken wildfowling by her two brothers, Geoff and Peter. It was a generous offer that I accepted with enthusiasm. The brothers were several years older than I and well versed in the ways of this potentially dangerous sport. Over three seasons, beginning in January 1937, they took me to Holy Island and the extensive area of tidal mudflats, known locally as the Slakes, which lie between it and the mainland, including Fenham Flats and Budle Bay. We used to stay at a small pub in Belford called The Black Swan, where we were given a bed and three excellent meals for 10/- (50p) each, which enabled us to fit in a morning and an evening flight. If the moon was favourable we would stay out for much of the night. From the Angus brothers I learned about tides, navigation in poor visibility, survival in extreme weather conditions and how to cross soft mud verging on quicksand, using wooden pattens roped to the feet of thigh waders. Wildfowling has always been a physically demanding sport, and the rougher the weather the better the prospects. The aim is always to reduce the distance between oneself and one's quarry, to get within effective range, and this involves fieldcraft, concealment, camouflage and, above all, local knowledge. Everything I was taught by the Angus brothers was invaluable training for the difficult conditions that I was to encounter in the future, and I also learned the caveat 'never go by night anywhere that you have not already been by day'.

In October 1938 I became an undergraduate at St John's College, Cambridge. Soon after arrival I met Charles Jewell, known to his close friends as Chips, who had just come up to Trinity College from Winchester. Through him I got to know his great friend Donald Campbell, and in February 1939 my friendship with these two Wykehamists led to a weekend wild goose chase on the Wash. When Chips and Donald invited me to accompany them I accepted with enthusiasm, being under the impression that between them they had enough knowledge and experience to meet our needs. Although I had never been to the Wash, I found the prospect exciting. After much planning and many preparations we set off on a Saturday morning in an old hired car and arrived at a farm near Holbeach, which was to be our base. It was bitterly cold and snowing sporadically. After some lunch we got ready and headed for the saltmarshes. On reaching the coastal embankment we looked out across the vast expanse of the Wash, which we knew extended beyond the horizon. As we expected, we found the tide out; it was not due to come in until after the evening flight. We continued across the foreshore towards a patch of marine vegetation about half a mile distant that would provide sparse cover. On the way we crossed three footbridges over deep creeks; night would come before our return, but the moon would be full and we anticipated no problems in finding our way back.

The idea was to intercept the geese, most of which were likely to be pinkfeet, on their return from their inland feeding grounds at dusk. We spread out about a hundred yards apart and waited. Beyond us, less than a quarter of a mile away, was a small wooden hut built on stilts which raised it at least fifteen feet, keeping it above the level of high tides. I learned later that this and one or two other distant huts were for observation purposes when the RAF bombing range farther out in the estuary was in use. Even in severe weather, this stage of the proceedings in wildfowling is full of anticipation and often magical in the beauty of sunrise or sunset, with the calling of curlews and other wading birds close at hand. Before long we picked up the distant chorus of the approaching geese, one of the most evocative sounds in the world of nature. However, as is so often the case, they passed wide of us. We gathered together and set off on our return to the foreshore as darkness fell.

Long before we were clear of the saltmarsh we suddenly became aware that we were being chased by the tide, an eventuality which had certainly not entered our minds. It soon caught up and overtook us as we ran clumsily towards the shore in our thigh boots and oilskins, laden with guns and cartridges. With the tide now ahead of us and rising all the time, we certainly had problems. The first was to find the bridges over the dykes, as night was closing in on the disappearing landscape. All traces of footpaths and dykes had vanished under the sea, but in the moonlight we were able to make out the handrails of each bridge as we approached it; although by the time we got to the third we were making slow progress and still had some way to go. Before long we realised that we were cut off from the shore. The tide had not only overtaken us but had outflanked us to a river bed, the sea level was rising fast and we were separated from the shore by well over a hundred yards of turbulent sea. "We'll have to swim", I shouted, preparing to discard my outer clothing. "Those who can", came the depressing answer, and it was clear we were up against it.

At this point a miracle occurred. Without warning or explanation a small empty rowing boat bore directly down on us on the strong tide as we struggled to keep our feet. We just managed to grasp it as it came level and heaved first our guns and then ourselves into it. When we realised there were no oars I left my legs in the water and paddled with them, holding on to the stern with my hands. The others used their guns to manoeuvre the boat. We soon met the strong side-current and were rapidly swept along parallel with the shore but, little by little, closed the gap until we reached land. Wet through and exhausted, we hauled the boat clear of the water and immediately found ourselves confronted by an incredulous farmer who had been on the look-out for us, having noted our outward journey several hours earlier. He was familiar with the ways of the Wash and assured us it had been the highest spring tide for five years. He could not account for the boat or even suggest how it came to be adrift. We thanked him for his concern for our wellbeing and made our way to the farm. Back at base we had a meal and no doubt some rum before we took stock of our situation. We were almost, if not entirely, wet through, living in a barn with no heat, one hurricane lamp, limited spare clothing and unlimited potato sacks. We had asked for nothing more, so we had no reason to complain and proceeded to make the best of it. My diary records a light-hearted discussion by the light of the solitary lamp on the merits of stripping down to underwear and relying on potato sacks for warmth, which was Donald's and my choice, or keeping everything on, dry or wet, which was Chips's intention. It seemed to make little difference; we all froze throughout the long and dreary night.

The following morning we concentrated on getting thawed out and dry, partially succeeding with the help of food and hot drinks. By early afternoon we were ready for another sally, having given much thought to the planning of it. We recognised how lucky we had been and were conscious of the need to avoid a repetition. The forecast was for a lower high tide nearly an hour later than the previous one, and to be confident of avoiding trouble we agreed to leave the saltings earlier, regardless of what sport we might be enjoying. We decided to move to the right of our former positions to improve our chances of getting under the flight-line. This would take us closer to the nearest 'bombing hut', and we would have a good route to follow all the way. Any experienced wildfowler will already be wondering how this story is going to work out. Had we taken account of wind conditions on the first night or the part they might play on the second? What safety margins had we allowed for the natural influences which affect tides? The answer is 'insufficient'. In defiance of the forecasts, the next tide was both earlier and higher than anticipated, and we were caught again. This time, in the light of our recent experience, we made for the hut, which we reached just in time and wet through once again. We scrambled the fifteen or more feet up the ladder and thankfully found the door at the top unlocked. Inside were one chair, a table and a broad shelf, presumably for maps and instruments. There were no means of communication and not even a candle. It was going to be a long night. When the moon rose we could see a vast expanse of sea on all sides and a few twinkling lights in the distance. It had become bitterly cold and before long came the first of the night's snow flurries. We had no food but a more than ample supply of rum, as it seemed that each of us had brought enough for all the party so there was a surplus to all reasonable requirements. This was almost the cause of our undoing and came close to ending what had, until then, been a promising friendship.

Several factors contributed to what followed: 1. No food. 2. Unlimited rum. 3. Zero temperature. 4. No light, other than from the moon. 5. Marooned with nothing to do. Gradually the rum took effect on the others as I adopted the role of onlooker, albeit just because I am not partial to rum and only drink it *in extremis*. As I began to feel the cold, despite a medicinal tot or two, the others perked up and began telling stories. Before long they were helpless with laughter, having a ball and no longer suffering from anything. The Wash had never seen two happier wildfowlers, and in this state, without conscious decision, they lay down on the floor and went to sleep. I was by now far too cold to sleep and concentrated on trying to keep some feeling in my limbs. What, until then, none of us had thought of for some time was to keep an eye on the sea level. When we had last taken note it was only a few feet up the ladder. But what was this gentle lapping sound against the timbers of the hut itself, rising above the heavy breathing from the floor? The moon helped to confirm that at any moment we were due to be joined in the hut by the North Sea, and the two prostrate bodies would become waterlogged. I sprang, if that is the right word, into action, shouting, pulling and eventually willing them into consciousness. Fortunately they responded, although it was a while before I had managed to assist one on to the table and the other on to the shelf, where they soon resumed the horizontal. Even so, I had to make sure they didn't roll off as I kept an eye on them from the chair. Meanwhile, the water level continued to rise, and before long I realised that, even when I had abandoned the chair, I was the most vulnerable of the three because the table and shelf were both quite a bit higher than the tops of my thigh boots. There was only one place to go and that was outside. From the open door I found hand- and footholds, with the aid of which I was able to pull myself up on to the flat roof. Once on top I could lie face down and, while leaning over the edge above the doorway, was able to look down into the hut and observe the motionless bodies, with the water still rising but with some way yet to go before it would reach them. Outside it froze and snowed; without protection I felt every gust of wind and began to lose the feeling in my limbs. There was nothing to do but stick it out. Before long I noticed that the water level had stopped rising, though it remained at its high tide mark for an interminable time. When it began to fall I was able to clamber down from the roof and put the whole process into reverse.

My two companions eventually woke out of their sound sleep, and by dawn we were able to make our way back to dry land, to the accompaniment of the geese leaving the saltings. I am glad to report that we encountered no search parties and in due course returned to Cambridge none the worse for our experience, though I hope a little wiser. We had shot neither geese nor duck, but would not have admitted to anyone that our weekend had been anything but enjoyable from start to finish. Our next visit was planned for 24/26 November 1939, but the War intervened and I never returned to the Wash. And, even after all this time, I still cannot provide any rational explanation for that oarless rowing boat, appearing in the dark from the North Sea at the very moment it was needed.

Chapter 3

'Paradise to a Shooter'

Although I was in the Army throughout the Second World War I was highly fortunate in the amount of game shooting that still came my way, both at home and overseas, and most of my records have survived, the exception being one notebook, which was destroyed by enemy action together with my shotgun in Holland in 1944. A recurring sporting problem during the War was the shortage of ammunition but, here again, I was fortunate in successive home appointments, first as a liaison officer and then as an instructor within the Reconnaissance Corps, both of which posts took me to many parts of both England and Scotland, travelling by road and free to vary my route. In 1830 there were apparently no fewer than 83 gunsmiths in London, and it was surprising, even more than a hundred years later, how many of the towns, large and small, through which I passed had gunsmiths or hardware shops which, in those days, sold guns and cartridges to all comers without restriction. My best source was the London gunsmith W. J. Jeffery, who had a commendable reputation for accepting guns of all grades from owners who no longer had any use for them. Somehow I had formed a personal relationship with the management and called in whenever I could, if only for a chat.

It so happened that during 1941, while I was stationed in the South of England, part of my time was spent in Dorset, on the outskirts of Poole and its extensive harbour. I was already familiar with the exploits there of Colonel Peter Hawker (1802-1853), who did a great deal of shooting around Poole, and before long I came to understand why so many wildfowlers regarded him almost as a patron saint. His *Diary*, in two volumes, first published in 1893, has become a classic and should be read by all shooting men. For my purpose one quotation from 7 December 1813 will suffice:

> Reached Poole, and proceeded to the 'Haven Passage House' where rooms were prepared for me, and round which the wild fowl were flying in hundreds, though too far for a shot. I could plainly see that if hard weather comes, this place will be a paradise to a shooter.

As my collection of guns for wildfowling increased so did the amount of time I had to spend dealing with the problems they presented, in order to enjoy using them. By the time I called a halt to acquisition my collection included 'Blitzer', a 4 bore weighing 19 lbs with a 46" barrel, 'Boanerges' (son of thunder), a double-barrel 8 bore, 'Bertha', a double-barrel 10 bore, and lastly a double-barrel 12 bore magnum, which in due course supplanted all the others. The larger guns gave me a lot of fun and killed many geese, but I never regretted my conversion to a magnum. In retrospect, perhaps the most interesting aspect of these purchases was the value for money that one took for granted in those days; similarly, when I had my car sent by rail from Newcastle to Poole it made the journey overnight for £4. At the time the purchase of the 10 bore clearly involved a certain amount of soul-searching, because I have a three-page letter written to my parents on 6 December 1942, when I was in Oxford attending a tactical course at Brasenose College, nearly all of which is about the possibility of acquiring another gun:

> Yesterday afternoon I had a good look round the shops in Oxford to try and buy a few Christmas presents for the family, but I could find nothing suitable for anyone. I shall try in London when I pass through at the end of the course. The only thing I saw and liked was another gun – I can hear you all saying, "What, hasn't he got enough already?"! Anyway, I haven't bought it, though I could if I allowed my will power to slacken. What I intend to do is to save up for it for a few months and buy it possibly in the spring if he still has it. I'll tell you about it. It is a 10 bore and though I have plenty of cartridges at home I have never had a 10 bore gun. I have seen many and this is by far the finest gun I have

ever seen. In the first place it is brand new – a pre-War Hardy. Second, and <u>most</u> uncommon, it is a hammerless ejector, the only one I have seen. The majority are hammer guns and very few are ejectors. It is in beautiful condition with 32" barrels, both well choked, and everything else as far as I can see is just as it should be. I asked him [the shopkeeper] what he wanted for it and he said £25, which is about half the price one would pay for it in London. I told him I didn't want it at all really, but if I should decide to buy it to put away until after the War, would he consider £20. He said yes he would as he had had it there since before the War and no one seemed to have any shells for it and he was fed up with the sight of it! He swore that it cost him £25 and that he would lose £5 on the deal, and I am almost inclined to believe him as before the War a third rate 12 bore would cost £20 and surely a 10 bore is much more expensive to produce. I've always understood so anyway. If I get it I shall have the complete battery – 4, 8, 10 and 12 magnum. What extravagance! Incidentally, he said I might have it on trial, so it would not be like buying a pig in a poke exactly. Tell me if you think it would be a sinful extravagance to buy it, say in 3 months. Then it would make it a bit longer since I bought a gun. And remember that Blitzer only cost me £6 and Boanerges £4:10:0 !

It was natural to find that the needs of the Services were paramount in wartime, and already sporting ammunition was less plentiful in the shops. Notwithstanding my contacts here and there, I felt it might be expedient to equip myself with the wherewithal for cartridge loading. The essential commodities were cases (often reused), caps, gunpowder and shot, all of which I found within the gun trade, and then I was in business, at least until the powder ran out. I was then fortunate in finding enough black powder to meet the requirements of my heavier pieces, and the column of flame and smoke that followed a shot was estimated by onlookers to be about thirty feet long. It was highly impressive after dark, and I became known as the chap who shoots with a flame gun. I often shot widgeon by night when there was enough moon showing to make it possible. After some years I had reached the stage, known to experienced wildfowlers, of relying as much on hearing as on sight when shooting duck by night. Eventually, for a minority of enthusiasts, hearing can predominate, unless there is much of a wind blowing, when the detection by sound alone of duck on the wing is no longer possible. In my case this stage lasted only as long as my hearing remained totally unimpaired, and sadly I became one of the many keen shooting men who shot before the 'ear-muff' era, as well as being one of a small number who were also blown up on mines during the War, so was doubly affected.

Undoubtedly, Poole featured in my wildfowling learning curve because it provided me with much useful experience in a setting that was quite different from those I already knew, and here I also learned to use a shotgun in the prone position. But, as is often the case, luck had much to do with it and it certainly played a major part in my introduction to punting for duck. In his *Instructions to Young Sportsmen*, first printed in 1814 and revised and published in 1830 with a dedication to HM William IV, Peter Hawker included full instructions and measurements for building a 'Poole Canoe for shooting from the creeks with a large shoulder gun'. Well did he deserve the title 'Father of Wildfowling'. It was in 1941, while I was engaged in my search for guns, that I came across just such a gunning punt lying in a Poole boatyard, where I was told that it was a Barnagate Bay 'sneak-boat' from the coast of New Jersey. It was thought to be the descendant of an original craft built on a scaled down plan of a Greenland whale-boat, though it only drew about two inches of water so was ideal for my purpose. Its owner, who had imported it before the War, had no further use for it, and I bought it for £2.

Once in possession of the punt I had to familiarize myself with it and its handling, for although I was used to recreational punting this was going to be very different. To begin with, it would necessitate lying down to adopt the lowest possible profile while paddling, concentrating on stealth and minimum movement within the craft in order to eliminate noise. According to the depth of water, which varied considerably, I had the choice of using pole or paddle to propel the punt until I sighted duck on the water, preferably with their attention elsewhere. Then I would adopt the prone position and limit myself to a single short paddle to stalk them. When I was confident in using the punt all I needed was to gain access to the large area of tidal marshland around Poole, where my unit was stationed. This was very close to the harbour, and I was delighted to find that we were within a mile or so of Brownsea Island, which was surrounded by an extensive area of wildfowl habitat. The threat of invasion had already necessitated the evacuation of civilians, and much of the coastal land had been classified as 'defence areas'. Part of it had become an artillery range, from which the public were excluded and within which live firing took place from time to time, but I felt it might be worth making some enquiries. Both the Army and the Navy seemed to have an interest in it, and by approaching those who had responsibility for the allocation of the range I discovered there would be a number of gaps from time to time when the range was not in use. There were also range wardens, one of whom befriended me and before long agreed to transport my punt to the far end of the training area, beyond the limit of the range. He warned me that it was my responsibility to ascertain that the range was not in operation before I set off to make use of my punt, and even then he seemed uneasy.

However, I decided to accept any risks and, in the meantime, after I had done my best to establish the times during which live firing would take place, discovered that the far end of the range was out of the target area; and there I found wildfowl that had reached the same conclusion. With the use of a bicycle to traverse the range I had some excellent sport, particularly with teal, though on one occasion I had to take cover when artillery started firing earlier than scheduled and shells landed too close for comfort. Even before I had started making use of the punt I had noticed an abundance of waterfowl round the remoter fringes of the harbour against which I was able to pit my wits, and this experience illustrated the value of a really good pair of binoculars, the importance of which was second only to a suitable gun.

On my last visit, as I was emerging from the training area, I was taken unawares by a staff car flying a two-star flag that stopped ominously beside me. I saluted the General sitting in the rear seat as well as I could with gun and all the encumbrances of a wildfowler about me, wondering how many transgressions I might be guilty of, but General Hayes, the District Commander, could not have been more charming or interested in my sporting endeavours. I almost offered him the teal I had shot, but felt this might be stretching a second lieutenant's licence a little too far. We parted on the best of terms and my memories of wildfowling in Poole harbour remained unblemished.

From Poole I was posted to Annan on the Solway Firth in order to join the instructional staff of the newly formed Reconnaissance Corps Junior Leaders School, conveniently arriving in late September, soon after the beginning of the shooting season. It was the beginning of a long and happy association with Dumfriesshire and the Solway, during which I had years of the best game shooting and wildfowling of my life. However, before I embarked on this inviting prospect, I was due for some home leave, which provided an ideal opportunity to rejoin my family and enjoy some partridge shooting with my father who, like my mother and all parents in time of war, looked forward to my visits, however brief. Plans were soon in place to provide such sport as was available, although that proviso hardly applied, because less of our shooting in those days was dependent on game management, largely due to the traditional pattern of farming with its regular rotation of cereal and root crops which ensured that partridges continued to prosper. These, of course, were native English grey partridges, redlegs at that time being unknown to most of our shoots, certainly in the North of England. My father's game book shows annual totals of grey partridges well into three figures, even during the war years, for an average of only two guns.

Recently I revisited some of these former haunts and spoke to two old inhabitants, who were able to confirm that coveys of native grey partridges can still be seen on the same land over which we shot more than seventy years ago, although they are not as numerous as they were then. On one of those wartime days, 20 October 1942, I used only home-loaded cartridges and was very pleased with the results, including the range at which they were effective against partridges, pheasants and even hares.

A feature of wartime shooting not prevalent otherwise was the inclusion of foxes in the bag. Although gamekeepers had always been keen to keep their numbers under control foxes had been traditionally reserved for hunting with hounds; but this was considerably reduced for the duration of the war, as a result of which few foxes were spared by shooting parties and virtually none by those gamekeepers still around. I have a diary entry for 20 March 1943, when I was a youthful Chief Instructor of the 3rd British Infantry Division Battle School located in Dumfriesshire, which reads: 'Moffat. This morning there was a large gathering of keepers and trappers in the town, all going out on a fox shoot – no bones made about it either.' An entry in my father's game book for 7 October 1943, while I was at home on a brief period of leave, records our bag as 10 partridges, 2 pheasants, 2 hares, 1 pigeon and, in the 'Various' column, 1 fox, although I cannot now remember which of us shot it. An earlier note in my father's game book in respect of a day's rough shooting reads: 'December 12th 1942. Very nice fine warm day. Pheasants were scarce and foxes plentiful.' This, of course, was consistent with the reduction in the number of gamekeepers, the younger ones having been called up for service in the Forces. However, not all shoots had ever employed regular keepers and, with vigilance, vermin could be kept reasonably under control. The small unkeepered shoot in County Durham where we shot as a family yielded 800 partridges and 468 pheasants during the seven years 1942-49. The seasonal bag for 1942/43 amounted to 106 Grey partridges, 63 pheasants, 1 woodcock, 17 hares and 14 rabbits. That year we also followed the wartime custom of shooting on Christmas Day.

Chapter 4

A Blizzard on the Solway

Before I arrived at Annan in September 1941 I was already familiar with the Solway's reputation among wildfowlers and was elated at the prospect of being stationed within a few hundred yards of the foreshore, though I was soon to discover that the best sport was usually to be had a few miles further west. What I had not anticipated was the hospitality offered by several private shoots on large estates in the neighbourhood, one of which still employed eight, albeit elderly, gamekeepers. Its owner was not only a very generous man, but took the view that although he himself was too old to serve his country in wartime he could still assist by providing sport for those of us with the requisite experience who were stationed nearby. He already knew our delightful commandant, Tom Welstead, who was a wonderful person and rode us with a light rein. He ran a most successful and happy school and ensured that almost all the instruction took place in the open countryside of Dumfriesshire, thus observing the maxim 'War is not fought in classrooms'. We had a generous allowance of recce vehicles and traversed the country in every direction, until those of us on the staff knew much of it as well as the natives, who could not have been more friendly. Tom knew many of the landowners personally and had served with several in the past. As a result, he being himself a keen shot, we soon had more invitations to shoot than we could accept. Tom was also aware of the Scottish sensitivity in those days and in some parts to recreational activities on the Sabbath, and one Sunday he asked me to accompany him to a meeting with the Provost.

The latter, I sensed, felt himself to be in a cleft stick: on the one hand he respected the reservations held by some of the older generation among the local inhabitants, while on the other were the interests of those entrusted with the defence of his portion of the realm, who had no such sporting inhibitions in wartime. We had, in fact, already played a keenly fought football match against a local team that morning, in which, incidentally, I had scored a goal. The Provost was anxious not to be associated with any protests and assured us that he had no 'perrrsonal' reservations concerning our recreation. Thereafter there was no further trace of embarrassment, and my association with the Solway developed into familiarity and, over many years, respect and affection for its inhabitants.

Because we were occupied with our students only by day, much of the remaining time was our own, and it was not long before some of us were enjoying the best wildfowling we had ever experienced, because so many of the resident wildfowlers were away on war service and most of those who had been visiting the Solway from any distance had insufficient petrol. As a result, we usually had the foreshore to ourselves whenever we chose to go. Before long, word of this paradise was passed by students to others in their regiments, who would bring their guns with them when their turn came to attend courses. One of these was Chips Jewell, whom I was able to introduce to the Solway as he had introduced me to the Wash. If my conscience about my frequent forays to the foreshore was ever uneasy, which I do not recall, I could have argued that my recreation was subjecting me to conditions far more rigorous than those of any Special Forces training programme. A contributory reason for these rigours was the wartime absence of any weather forecasts, because of the value these would have had to the *Luftwaffe*. The BBC referred to the weather only in past terms. A more practical point in favour of the use of rod and gun was the benefit which both brought to the kitchens and menus of all ranks, at a time when food was not plentiful.

It therefore became my practice throughout that season to set off from Annan to our favourite stretches of foreshore whenever possible, using whatever mode of transport was available and accompanied by my Labrador, Dinah. An important aspect of my shooting before, during and ever since the Second World War, has been the presence, or very rarely absence, of a Labrador. It was a great day in 1936 when my mother was given a black bitch pup by a grateful master of foxhounds for whom she had walked a succession of hound puppies. The pup was given the name of Dinah, and eleven generations later of the same line of black Ds we now have Diri, who is as good as any of her forebears, with the single exception of Dinah herself, who was in a class of her own. My father already had a shooting dog, a lovely spaniel named Sam, so my mother gave Dinah to me, and whenever I was stationed in the British Isles she accompanied me. Not only was she a wonderful companion for me, but the problem of feeding a dog during the War was eased, because there were always scraps left over in the cookhouse.

Gradually I built up a network of friendly farmers who would let me know the latest flightlines of the greylag and pink-footed geese as they flew at dawn from their roosting sandbars, often far out in the estuary, to inland feeding areas, and then back again at dusk. By night duck, mainly widgeon, would traverse the salt marshes below the high water mark, and when the moon was favourable these would keep any keen fowler out of his bed. My favourite starting point was Stanhope Farm at the mouth of the River Lochar. Here the Scott family was most hospitable and bade me call in whenever I was in need of sustenance, thawing or drying out. If ever I wished a bed and meals, they too were provided. Towards the end of October 1941 I had the opportunity I had been waiting for, to fit in a dawn flight at Stanhope. As I waited, the first skeins of greylag geese approached, and I stared in wonder as between two and three thousand flew inland, many overhead though out of range. This was a completely new experience, and I became captivated by the spectacle and the chorus, which thrilled me as nothing in nature had ever done before. It has continued to have the same effect on me to this day, and though I do not live close to a flight-line, sometimes by night geese pass over my house on migration. My bedroom window will be flung open, whatever the hour, and my thoughts take me back to the Solway, with memories of days and nights in pursuit of greylag, pink-footed and barnacle geese.

As often as not it was bitterly cold, but the fouler the weather the better the prospects. Wildfowling has its own rugged enchantment for those who are prepared to accept its discomforts, hardships and occasional dangers in return for the anticipation and the magical sights and sounds of remote places. Bags, thankfully, are usually small, but full of interest and variety, bearing no comparison with those of game shooting. I no longer care for the statistical approach to shooting, whether it relates to nature's limited resources or to the unlimited stocks of gamebirds reared by those obsessed with the size of their bags. My collection of old shooting registers, notebooks and diaries covering eighty-five years of my own sport I now view with mixed feelings, but relish the memories of far off days when it was the variety of the bag rather than its size which mattered. On 5 November 1941 I shot three greylags during the morning flight, and two more four days later. On 17 November I celebrated my first right and left at pink-footed geese and by then I was recording, 'There are more geese than ever, many thousands.' My game book entry that shows the greatest variety also reflects the contribution of Dinah and an anecdote which became known to the family as 'Dinah's Seal'.

The background to this was the wartime problem that fishermen were experiencing of seals forcing their way into nets holding fish. As a result, wildfowlers were asked to shoot any seals when they had an opportunity and were advised to use SSG shot for the purpose. In due course I was able to do just that, but had not foreseen Dinah's reaction: to exercise her rightful prerogative of using her initiative to retrieve everything I shot when wildfowling. On this occasion I was unable to restrain her as she plunged into the creek, undeterred by the seal which was in its death throes. Although it was at least equal to her in weight she grasped it by a flipper and, half pushing, half pulling, brought it ashore. My bag for that flight was: 1 pink-foot, 2 widgeon, 1 mallard, 1 shelduck, 1 coot and 1 seal!

When I came to know the Lochar, the ways of the Solway tides and the treacherous mud in some of its creeks, I used to cross the river at low tide, either before or after the evening goose flight, with the intention of spending the night out on the 'merse', which is now part of the Caerlaverock Nature Reserve. On these occasions it was necessary to have the prospect of some moonlight. The main drawback to this plan was that it involved becoming marooned by the rising tide, with no alternative but to remain on the salt marsh for most or all of the night, totally exposed to the elements. Shades of the Wash!

Such a night was that of Saturday 31 January 1942, with a strong wind and the temperature below freezing. A full moon was about to rise as I waded in my thigh boots across the mouth of the Lochar, fifty yards or more wide. By following the shallower, diagonal course one could make it at low tide without going over the tops of one's waders, but the river level was an important part of the equation and many were the wettings. My companion, as usual, was Dinah. I made this first crossing of the evening without taking in water, and with Dinah, who had no choice, swimming by my side. Prospects were excellent, with reports of thousands of geese flighting over Stanhope for some days past, but, as is so often the way of it, they eluded me and the evening flight was a washout. We recrossed the Lochar at about 9.00 pm for supper at Stanhope, and this time I went in over the tops of my waders so there were two of us to dry, Dinah being the easier.

After supper we set off again and spent the next few hours stalking geese without success – they are very wary and always have sentinels on the alert. It was just after midnight and perishingly cold when, quite suddenly, it began to snow. On this my diary records, 'It has snowed non-stop ever since and is still snowing as I write nearly 24 hours later'. While I could still see I shot a mallard which fell into the Lochar, and Dinah made a splendid retrieve. Soon after that my gun jammed with snow as I attempted to shoot at a single goose which nearly took my cap off, followed by a whole flock of greylags which passed low over me. The jam righted itself as soon as the geese were out of range. By now I was feeling the effects of the wind and low temperature, and so was Dinah, who had already had several swims in the freezing water. However, before long a pack of barnacle geese came flying up the river and I dropped two into it. Dinah entered the water again for the fifth time, swimming against the tide which was now high, and after about five minutes returned, carrying one of the two geese. The other had disappeared in the snow and darkness, being rapidly swept up the Lochar.

I have always allowed my wildfowling dogs to decide when and what to retrieve, because their hearing and eyesight are so much better than ours. They make these decisions, not I; however, that does make it difficult, if not impossible, to stop them when conditions are dangerous. By now we were both in poor shape, and as my diary records: 'It was still blowing hard and snowing heavily and the rest of the night was most uncomfortable' – which I now concede is something of an understatement. I then noted:

Eventually I started to lose all feeling in my fingers, arms and legs. I staggered about the creeks to keep my circulation going and every now and again went through the ice and snow into the running water below. My gloves got wet with the snow which was still coming down and then froze to my hands. The duck came over, but I was too cold to get the gun up in time. Then the geese came. I just could not find the trigger and time and again they streamed over unfired at. I was almost in tears until eventually I found I had enough feeling to pull the trigger and dropped one pinkfoot in the snow out of a bunch of about 30 which came straight at me, very low. I continued to miss them, owing to the cold and bad shooting.

In fact it was Dinah who helped me through the remainder of the night and played a critical part in my survival. We were now in a real blizzard, and conditions ensued the like of which I have never experienced before or since. My only waterproof garment was a loose-fitting Army gas-cape of thin fabric, but this gave me a useful idea. Lying on my side in the snow with my back to the wind, I coaxed Dinah to join me and soon was able to button up the cape with her inside it next to me. She was wringing wet but lay quite still, and before long I was benefiting from her body heat, which in dogs is several degrees higher than in humans. We lay like this for several hours as the snow piled up on top of us, and although my extremities were frozen, my body felt as though it had a tepid hot-water bottle next to it, albeit a very wet one.

My wildfowling notebook for that season contains a seven-page entry about this episode in the lives of a man and his dog, towards the end of which comes the following passage: 'I reckon I should have shot 12 geese altogether during the night and morning if I had not been using a gun on trial and had some rum and more clothing. However, I had gathered 2 geese and 1 mallard, and lost one goose and one duck, so I couldn't complain.' Seventy years later, what I remember most clearly and what really mattered was the part played by Dinah.

Postscript: When I had finished writing the above account, using my original records, I wondered if it might have been unduly influenced by my physical reactions to the weather, so I consulted the Meteorological Office for verification, and a helpful member of staff unearthed a copy of the monthly weather reports for January and February 1942. The report for January was headed: 'Cold; mainly dull; considerable snow', and began, 'The weather was unusually cold, with severe frost.' The report for February stated, 'The month was remarkable for its persistently cold character ... over Scotland generally it was the coldest February since 1900 and over England and Wales since 1895.'

Chapter 5

Wildfowling Reverie

The man who shoots his first wild goose with little or no positive effort misses much pleasure. Never does he know the feelings of excitement and triumph that come after months, or even years, of fruitless effort and patience, to say nothing of discomfort, when, at last, we are rewarded with success. To the fowler, his first goose is a landmark never to be forgotten in a sporting life, and well may it be compared with the deer stalker's first stag or the salmon angler's first fish.

I wrote the above in 1943, on a small sheet of flimsy blue paper, and recently came across it when sorting through old records. It was possibly inspired by my return to the Solway in 1943 and the self-imposed task of helping a friend, Guy Thornycroft, who had been a few years senior to me at Shrewsbury School and was now a fellow instructor at the 3rd British Infantry Division Battle School. I was fortunate in having been introduced to wildfowling as a boy and later, having fallen under its spell, I came to regard it as having no equal among all other field sports of my experience. Guy had also become fascinated by wildfowling, but was one of many fowlers who knew the bitterness and exasperation of continual defeat at the hands of the *Anser* species. Year after year, on one estuary or another, he had been taunted by wild geese until eventually, as far as this sport was concerned, he proclaimed himself as being jinxed. And so it was that we found ourselves stationed within easy reach of one of the best wildfowling estuaries in Britain. I knew it well and sang its praises to Guy, who had never shot there, but although he was duly impressed he still feared a repetition of his former bad luck. He was so convinced of this that rashly I promised to ensure that he would shoot his first goose before the end of the year. What an unwise thing to say, considering the uncertainties of the sport, even on such an estuary as the Solway!

Guy accepted the challenge with enthusiasm, and we laid our plans. In spite of the many difficulties, not the least of which was an intensification of our invasion training, we thought we might manage three short visits to the estuary before Christmas. The first day was 9 November, and we arrived for the evening flight in high spirits, having arranged to stay at the farm I knew well. That first night was hopeful, and in spite of the calm weather we gathered six widgeon. The following morning we tried for a goose, for that was the object of the trip, but Guy's bad luck persisted and, although we saw a large number, we did no good.

During the day the weather changed and the sky became overcast. As the dark clouds gathered and the wind rose it became obvious that 'fowlers' weather' was on the way. By the afternoon there was a strong gale in full blast, and rain came with it that turned to a downpour. At 5.00 pm we left the farm and struck out into the gale. By then it was blowing with hurricane force, and the driven rain came lashing down in torrents. As we crossed the saltings it was hard to stay on our feet and, in spite of allowing an hour more than the previous day, we were too late to see the start of the flight. While it was still quite light the duck had been driven in from the sea, and as we advanced we could see them carpeting the saltings in front of us. As we came within a hundred yards of them they rose in a cloud, only to wheel round, almost unable to battle against the gale, and pitch again quite close. Never had we seen duck like this and never had either of us shot in such conditions. More duck streamed in from the sea and hurtled past us at terrific speed; I hit one and had to run 300 yards downwind to gather it, and this was the form for the rest of the flight. When we reached our creeks we were in the thick of it, but conditions were enough to baffle even the most experienced. Shot birds were torn from us by the gale, which took everything before it, and then it became like a bad dream; the air was full of duck but our cartridges were wet, our fingers were frozen and our guns became affected by particles of mud from our hands and oilskins. Guy's gun was so bad that he had to return to the farm to free it with a cleaning rod, while I struggled at the bottom of my creek; so we lost valuable time.

At last, as darkness fell, the storm died down and the flight was over. The conditions had even defeated Dinah, as duck that fell downwind of me continued to roll across the merse before the force of the tempest. Dinah at first found it confusing, for while she was in the act of retrieving one duck another would be blown past her. However, she worked tirelessly and showed the qualities which made her the outstanding Labrador among all those I have owned. One or two of those qualities might have been regarded by some as amounting to common sense, which in animals we describe as instinct. When a wounded duck made for the protection of a neighbouring watercourse she seemed to sense its intentions and then thwart them. If she suspected there were further wounded ducks at large she intensified her search without waiting to be sent, and there were instances when she appeared to be emulating the best of spaniels. Such initiative in a dog is, in my view, commendable, and even experienced guns may do well to recognise that in some situations dogs can, if only occasionally, know best. That night on the Solway with Dinah's assistance we gathered fourteen duck and had to leave others that had been swept away into the water. As we walked back to the farm, drenched to the skin, we discussed in tones of awe how many we might have got if only …

We were unable to arrange another visit until 11 December. Time was getting short and still Guy had not got his goose. We arrived for the evening flight and crossed on to the saltings full of hope, after hearing optimistic reports from the farmer. We were 400 yards apart, and as it got darker I lost sight of Guy in his hide. Most of the geese came back that night on another line, but I heard several flying towards Guy and in the darkness two flashes from his gun told me they had been within range. I continued my vigil and shot a few duck, but no geese came over me. As soon as the flight finished I hurried over to join Guy. "Did you, er … ?" I started to ask, rather hesitantly. "Yes, I did," he replied, rather as if he had been doing it all his life, and held up his first goose, a greylag. Then he told me how he had missed with his first shot but dropped his goose behind him at extreme range with his second. We were both well aware of the magnitude of the occasion as we returned to the farm, and certainly the five duck we had also collected sank into insignificance beside this fine gander.

Guy had lifted the jinx, and we carried his first goose back in triumph. Perhaps it was as well that the visit had ended in such success, because only the previous day I had emerged from hospital after a severe bout of 'flu and had then proceeded to do everything I should not have done under the circumstances. I had got wet and cold and had stood about like the ass I undoubtedly was, and the fact that I failed to get pneumonia is quite inexplicable. Perhaps any ill effects were staved off by the subsequent celebration the same evening on return to the Mess. The look on the face of the Commanding Officer (not himself a wildfowler), as he came in late and saw the cause of the gaiety propped up on the mantelpiece as though stuffed, was not the least amusing feature in an evening rather full of such incidents.

Ten days later, on 21 December, came the third and last of these memorable days. Guy and I arrived in time for the evening flight, having arranged to stay until the following morning. The flight was a race against time and tide, but even so we conducted a successful engagement with a large pack of barnacle geese, and Guy chalked up his first of that species. After supper and the night at the farm we were in position for the flight the next morning before the first flush of dawn appeared in the sky. We listened to the chorus from the geese out on the mud flats and as it grew light we watched them rise and wing their way inland in great straggling skeins. I was badly placed for the flight, but had the pleasure of seeing Guy topple out of the sky his first of yet another species of wild goose, as a pinkfoot crashed down into stubble behind him. Surely the jinx was lifted with a vengeance! The New Year saw me far from Dumfriesshire, heading for Haifa in Palestine and a very different landscape. However, despite, or perhaps because of, the privations of wartime life, the forays I enjoyed on the Solway, alone or in company and invariably with Dinah, have remained as bright jewels in the memory.

Chapter 6

Chancing it in No-Man's-Land

Following the successful Allied invasion of Normandy in the summer of 1944, the British Second Army broke through the German defences and fought its way out of France, through Belgium and into Holland, where it reached the River Maas before the onset of winter. There both sides defended their respective banks of the river, which was some 250 yards wide, in a winter vigil which lasted four months. In the meantime I had arrived from the Eighth Army in Italy to take command of 'A' Squadron of the Third Reconnaissance Regiment, which had become responsible for the defence of several villages set back from the river on raised ground, its three squadrons sharing a river frontage of some four miles of relatively open farmland. There the armoured cars were in control by day until dusk, when they were withdrawn for the night, leaving a wide expanse of low lying land nominally in our hands, though lightly held. This area included an attractive choice of wild duck flight-lines between the river and the cornfields behind us that had been sown earlier in the year, before the tide of war suspended farming activity, but had not been harvested. The duck at that time were in no danger of being shot, because apparently in May 1940 most firearms and ammunition in Holland had been impounded by the Germans, as the occupying power, and most, if not all, game shooting had ceased as a result.

We had not been there for long before I noticed that after sunset there was a period of aerial activity as flights of mallard came off the fringes of the river to a pond just beyond our forward positions. The whole area was also ideal shooting country, with plenty of partridges and hares in evidence. A few sporting enthusiasts in our ranks had had the foresight and opportunity to stow a shotgun in their vehicles before D-Day, but unfortunately I had been unaware of the possible need for such a weapon in North West Europe and had had no opportunities for using one in Italy. However, quite soon after my arrival my duties brought me into close contact with a Dutch police officer, whom I was able to assist over one or two internal security problems. As we got to know each other he noticed my interest in the duck, and I must have mentioned how much I regretted not having been able to bring my shotgun with me. Very soon I was able to report an exciting development in a letter to my parents:

> The big news of the week is the fact that I am now the proud possessor of a 12 bore which I have named 'Uncle Kit'. [A favourite elderly relation who in later life cherished an ancient piece.] It is what I would call 'post flintlock', but would go no further. I bought it for £2 from a Dutch police inspector who also gave me 25 German cartridges for it. It is, needless to say, a hammer gun, non-ejector, under-lever and its ancient barrels were woefully rusted. However, my armourer corporal stripped it down, took most of the muck and rust out and made it tolerably safe to let off. I did so tonight and am still whole. I took it out for half an hour after tea and had one shot at a rabbit which I missed. There are also some partridges about and I have been greatly tantalised by them recently. Of all game birds guess what I flushed the other day? A Greyhen! And no shadow of doubt. It got up at my feet out of a small patch of heather. I wonder how many of our sportsmen know there are heather and Blackgame in Holland.

As soon as I had a shotgun I was able to enhance the prospect of sport that the mallard offered by the judicious distribution of rotten potatoes rejected by the squadron cooks, and the skins from those peeled for consumption. The timing of this duck feeding, which was followed at intervals by a duck flight, was critical. If too early in the evening one was liable to draw enemy machine gun or even artillery fire. That was resented as much by the duck as by those in pursuit of them, and they might be frightened off for several days. There was therefore a window of opportunity at dusk, when visibility restricted the view from the enemy's Observation Posts and our patrols were not yet out because they would be vulnerable in the open during this period of stand-to. That was the time to be out with a shotgun and, having full responsibility for what went on within my sector, I was free to take advantage of it whenever I chose. On such occasions I would be considered to be 'off duty', and the second-in-command or another officer took over.

Before I went out on my game shooting forays I had realised that it was necessary, on grounds of both safety and common sense, to ensure that all members of my squadron were aware of their commander's periodical aspiration to shoot duck on our right flank, just outside our perimeter, between dusk and nightfall. At the least it saved them from the inconvenience of having to 'stand to' if some inconclusive report came in of shooting nearby. However, notwithstanding this precaution, from time to time the squadron's routine 'state of alertness' was activated by someone who lacked the necessary information about my movements; but I hope any annoyance was counteracted by the subsequent addition to the rations.

When the chance came, so did the feelings of magical anticipation known to all committed wildfowlers. Waiting in expectation is the essence of this sport wherever it is pursued. Nor at this time was I a lone spirit, because one or two friends with whom I had already shot in the United Kingdom were then serving in the same division, although this time we were shooting independently when opportunities arose. Guy Thornycroft, then commanding a company, had obviously been well prepared for a range of operational and sporting situations, having had a long metal box attached to the front bumper of his Jeep, containing a service rifle, a .22 rifle and a shotgun. Each had its purpose and all were effectively used according to the needs of the moment. Others serving in the Third Infantry Division had also found a means of bringing their shotguns for use if and when it was possible. Several of them became casualties before they had had the chance to use their sporting weapons, and a brigade commander in our division was seriously wounded by a mine while shooting partridges in Holland. However, he was unlucky, and his misfortune did not deter the rest of us when we saw opportunities to use our shotguns. There is no doubt that one did take a chance now and again, perhaps in the belief that life was apt to be rather full of risks at the time and if one was going to be unlucky one might as well have a shotgun in one's hands as anything else. My own indiscretions were, I must admit, numerous, but I hope without foolhardiness.

Although we usually managed to keep our sporting forays separate from operational activity this was not always possible, due to enemy intervention. On Guy Fawkes night in 1944 I was returning in the dark from an evening flight rather later than usual when I met a stretcher-party from my squadron evacuating a casualty. I followed them so that I could have a word with the wounded man before he was driven, secured on to a Jeep, to a field dressing station. At this point he held out a hand with the request, "Sir, will you please look after this." In the dark I did not know for what I was to become responsible and was somewhat surprised to find it was a No. 36 H E grenade. As the story circulated round my squadron that evening it became embellished by the addition of 'with the pin out', and so it was reported in the following day's news sheet! War without humour would be a much grimmer business than it is, certainly in the British Army.

From time to time during that memorable winter we were withdrawn from our exposed role overlooking the River Maas for a period of rest and recuperation away from the river. It was during one of those rest periods, on 4 December, that a friend and I had one of those shooting days that remain vivid in the memory long after most others have faded. At all events it served to feature as the main item in my next letter home, which recorded my impressions in some detail, beginning thus:

> Two days ago my second-in-command and I spent an afternoon partridge shooting. He has found another 'Uncle Kit' and I took out the original on what turned out to be a most entertaining day.

I went on to describe how our attached Dutch interpreter, at my suggestion, had contacted a local gamekeeper who, like most others at that time, had lost his job but agreed to seek out a few willing locals to act as beaters while we shot partridges. In no time we had many more beaters than we actually needed, and the situation was in danger of getting out of hand. We were also having problems of communication, being dependent on an interpreter who was a stranger to the countryside, let alone its sporting activities and traditions.

Eventually we moved off, with the intention of walking up a few partridges, but were soon caught up and overtaken by the beaters with their dogs, everyone in the best of humour. Almost as an afterthought one of them, who could speak a little English, sensing our puzzlement, turned back and explained what was going on. He and his friends, together with their motley pack of dogs, were heading for the large wood in the distance in order to draw it for hares, apparently in the knowledge that the wood was full of them. For our benefit they intended to drive it as systematically as a hare drive permits, from one side of the wood to the other, and if we went with him he would place us in positions from which we might have a good chance of a shot or two as hares emerged from cover. That is more or less what happened, as we were introduced to our first (and only) 'beagle-shoot', which I believe the French would have described as 'une grande chasse'. My second-in-command and I did both manage to shoot a hare, although so close behind them was the pack of dogs in full cry that only the exhortation of the hunt followers persuaded us to shoot at all. After a final exchange of compliments we parted, the 'field' returning to the realities of 'Starvation Winter', and my friend and I going back to duty.

Just before Christmas the temperature began to drop with a vengeance, and by the first week of the New Year it had descended to 10°F, which was exceptionally low for that part of Western Europe, even during that bitter winter. Our routine was disrupted when tracked vehicles froze to the ground with locked brakes which had to be freed by the use of blowlamps. The duck were numerous and found their natural feeding grounds unyielding, so came even more readily to the scraps we left out for them. Thereafter it became a matter of deciding when and how to shoot them and, more importantly, when to desist, particularly at a time when the enemy held an area on our side of the river, separated from us only by a tributary, from which they could harass our open flank. My letter home that week reflected my level of enthusiasm:

I started with about 4 Mallard and by visiting them every afternoon with half a sack of rotten potatoes or corn they multiplied quickly and I planned to shoot them on our last night. [We were due to hand over to another squadron.] Unfortunately on the night before the shoot was planned an enemy patrol came up the stream and the result was they [duck] were disturbed and left at once. They were absent the whole of the next day and when I went along for the evening flight there was a very thick fog. However, they started to trickle in as it got dusk and I dropped three, gathering two. Not wishing to have an enemy patrol to contend with as well I retired before the end of the flight. I enjoyed it thoroughly and we ate the duck in a few days' time.

Looking back at this period of my wartime service, much of my shooting was 'for the pot', as a means of supplementing our wartime rations. In such circumstances there is more satisfaction than enjoyment when a foray is successful, and for those few who thought it worthwhile, perhaps the most abiding memory is of the pain, not just discomfort, of shooting in temperatures of 10°F, or 22 degrees of frost.

The main tactical complication of which I needed to be aware was that, as mentioned, on the flank of our position on the river front the enemy held an enclave on 'our' bank of the Maas, and we were only separated by the Molenbeek, a narrow tributary of the main river. However, both sides appeared to have reached the same conclusion, that there would be no advantage in attempting to outflank the other beyond this feature. I hoped my confidence was not misplaced in thinking that no enemy would visualise any threat from a British sportsman using a shotgun within his own territory. But it did occur to me that the Germans might consider I was cocking a snook, would resent it and therefore contemplate counter-measures. I kept this in mind, but I also had a feeling that among all the Germans who must have realised just what was going on close by, there might have been some sportsmen who would be envying me, armed with a shotgun for sporting use. Was it entirely coincidental, I later wondered, that during none of my duck flights was there any interference or reaction from the enemy?

In the intervening years my memories of shooting in no man's land have never faded, and from time to time I still wonder what the Germans with whom we shared much of the River Maas thought of those of their adversaries who chose to spend so many cold evenings sporting with shotguns. During the eight weeks of our Maas vigil when shooting was possible I was fortunate in getting forty-one partridges and seven hares; but I have no records of duck because sadly the grimmer side of war intervened some time later when my armoured car was knocked out by a German Panzer. I had just climbed out, but my driver and wireless operator were killed and my shot gun and duck-flighting notebook were destroyed.

Chapter 7

Sandgrouse beyond Beersheba

Palestine in 1945 was a vibrant country that Britain had administered since 1923 under a Mandate of the League of Nations. It had become an established peacetime station for the British Army which, in conjunction with the Palestine Police, was responsible for the maintenance of law and order. Although overshadowed by internal conflict, as a military posting it had many advantages, one of which was almost unlimited sport when off duty.

My regiment, as part of 6th Airborne Division, had sailed from Glasgow on the troopship *Cameronia* in October, taking ten days to arrive at Haifa. We had an uneventful voyage, during which those of us on board who were interested in birds were able to observe many species that joined the ship as migrants for at least part of the journey, according to its course and their inclinations. These included quails, turtledoves, wagtails, chaffinches, flycatchers and even robins. Once an unidentified bird of prey circled round the ship, but declined to join us.

From Haifa we travelled south by train, down most of the length of Palestine with the Mediterranean Sea on our right, as far as Gaza, close to the Egyptian border. Two miles south of the town, close to the sea, we found our empty campsite, which had a water supply as its sole facility. Tents were soon delivered, and before long we discovered that night-time pilferage at the hands of highly expert Arab thieves was a constant threat, though it diminished and was eventually eradicated as we improved our security. As soon as the campsite was established, training for our strategic role took priority, although time was set aside for recreation, with sea-bathing initially the universal choice towards the end of what had been a hot summer. Unfortunately, there were dangerous currents and these, coupled with the approach of winter, mild though it was, imposed restrictions; but before then the Division lost several men through drowning.

Meanwhile, those of us who had brought our shotguns with us were on the lookout for opportunities to use them. I had already learned the importance of keeping a shotgun with me on active service, and within days of our arrival we were making plans to occupy our free time. Thirty miles to the south-east of our camp lay the small, historic, southern desert town of Beersheba, with which we would soon become familiar as it lay on the route to excellent sandgrouse terrain. At that time the town consisted of mud-brick dwellings with only a few modern buildings. Camel and sheep rearing prospered, and it was a centre for the semi-nomadic Bedouin tribes that inhabited the area. The local population was less than four thousand, of whom most were Muslims, with a small number of Christian Arabs. Two years later the 1947 United Nations Partition Plan allotted Beersheba to the Arab state because the population was almost exclusively Arab. However, by the turn of the century the population had grown to over 150,000 and was 99% Jewish. The sheep and camels had been replaced with electronics and chemical plants, and the residential area had the tallest apartment building in Israel outside Tel Aviv. But that was all unimaginable to us as we got to know the people and the surrounding land bordering Palestine's southern desert, known as the Negev. This is comprised largely of stony hills, fissured by numerous deep wadis, known mainly to nomadic tribesmen. To the south lay the vast Wadi Araba, stretching to the Gulf of Aqaba.

While we were settling into our camp near Gaza we were visited by the District Commissioner of the Gaza District, Palestine then being divided into six districts. The town when we knew it was peaceful and prosperous, and my impression as a newcomer was one of stability. However, it has a long history as a fortress and had been besieged and sacked by many conquerors, including Alexander the Great, Pompey and Napoleon, More recently, Allenby had contributed to the strategic importance of this small settlement. The District Commissioner was friendly and helpful, and it was through him that I met Sami Khrayl, who belonged to one of Gaza's leading families. Before long

Sami had become a friend, partly through his love of sporting guns. His father was the proud owner of an English gun, though he seldom used it. They both accompanied us on our first sporting foray, but it was Sami who became our guide and shooting mentor.

I was commanding a squadron of the divisional reconnaissance regiment that had recently come under command of a charming, but eccentric, cavalry officer of Swedish descent. Although he had some of the more orthodox qualities for command, his interest and expertise in jazz and conducting the regimental dance band, comprised mostly of national servicemen, too often took priority over his more important responsibilities. On the other hand, he did own a shotgun and was anxious to use it. When he became aware of my interest in the sport he appointed me regimental 'shooting officer'. This suited me well because with it went the right to use regimental transport whenever I wished, to carry out unlimited reconnaissance or take parties out on 'recreational training'. A 'party' consisted of not fewer than two participants, and it was not long before recreational shooting had no restrictions apart from obtaining the approval of a superior officer. The final stage soon followed, which allowed recreational shooting to take place whenever duties permitted, and the next three years provided opportunities for some of the best sport of my life.

We discovered almost immediately that it was, in late October, still legal to shoot sandgrouse, and subsequently I was amused to find that this species in which we were interested had come into season on 12 August. One did not need to be a knowledgeable ornithologist to realize that none of the reasons for the lawful start of grouse shooting in the United Kingdom could possibly apply thousands of miles away in the Middle East. Was it, I wondered, due to a lack of or a surfeit of imagination, or just the sense of humour, of some senior British Army officer or member of the High Commission in Jerusalem, which had prompted the choice of that date, unconnected as it was with the breeding season and circumstances of sandgrouse? I never discovered.

Anyway, it took some of us only three days to settle into our campsite before our vanguard of five shooting enthusiasts, headed by the Colonel and including the second-in-command, set off on Friday 26 October for our first sandgrouse shoot, accompanied by Sami and his father. This was only four days after we had disembarked at Haifa, and none of us had even seen a sandgrouse before, but we soon became familiar with them. The Arabs referred to them onomatopoeically as 'ghatta', from the sound they utter in continuous chorus when on the wing. There was no local ornithologist to consult, but from photographs I took at the time and subsequent research it appears that of the five species of the bird that existed then within the catchment area of the River Jordan, the one that provided us with our best sport was the black-bellied, sometimes called the 'imperial' sandgrouse. It is a pretty, fawn-coloured bird with mottled markings, about the size of a partridge.

On the day before our initiation, Sami had stressed the importance of being in our positions, to which he would escort us, in time to be settled by 8.30 am when, according to him, the first sandgrouse would be approaching our wadi, the only one in the area that had not dried out due to lack of rain. The sandgrouse would have been searching for grain since dawn and then be seeking water. I was impressed by Sami's exactitude, but assumed that it was his way of ensuring that we would be there in good time. He need not have worried because we rose at 5.15 am and, once we had collected Sami, were clear of Gaza and heading for Beersheba, the Colonel took the lead. Our progress then became like the driving of Jehu and possibly across the same territory that Jehu traversed so furiously. We were travelling in Jeeps, and although the road from Gaza to Beersheba was metalled we soon left it to drive on a rough track for a good half hour, eventually arriving at the upper reaches of Wadi Gaza where a small trickle of water flowed down the river bed. Here it was easy to imagine the feelings of T. E. Lawrence as he crossed the same terrain by camel in the First World War while organising the Arab Revolt against the Turks in 1916. In *Seven Pillars of Wisdom* he wrote: 'The coming of spring made the first part of the ride along the edge of the Araba scarp surprisingly beautiful.' I was also impressed by the number of nomads that we met following their traditional way of life, as though in a time warp. At first the bird life was limited, although I did observe three varieties of vulture. I recorded later my feeling that I would never repeat this experience, and so it has proved.

It was in fact precisely at half past eight, by which time we were waiting concealed behind large rocks, that I became aware of a faint ripple of sound coming from far away and still, I estimated, some miles to the east of us. Gradually I got the impression of a distant chorus, the like of which I had never heard before; but as it increased in volume I sensed it must come from the sandgrouse for which we were waiting. In this state of expectation I had the same feeling of excitement I associated with the first appearance of red grouse on the moors at home that I had known since boyhood. When the sandgrouse came into sight they were flying much higher and a lot faster than I had anticipated. They approached us in such numbers that I was taken by surprise, for they were grouped into close coveys of a score or more, sometimes expanding into packs as the scores multiplied into hundreds. As they came within range of the guns, who were dispersed over a wide area, most of us were soon in action and firing as fast as we could reload. However, despite their numbers, which before long reached many hundreds and continued to increase until I was convinced they were well into four figures, most birds were flying at a height that presented challenging shots. On this first occasion we were unprepared for the rapid rate of firing and soon had barrels that were too hot to hold. Thereafter, locally made crude gloves were brought into use, until a supply of specialist hand-guards arrived from England. These could be fitted to the barrels and solved the problem; I doubt if more than a few of our number had ever previously encountered this need.

Our bag for this first sandgrouse shoot was fifty-eight in two hours. When we finished shooting, Arabs appeared as though by magic quite close to us from the rocks around and joined in the fun with great humour. They were genuine desert Bedouins, still carrying their knives and long swords, and all very cheerful. They were not there when we arrived and we had not been aware of any movement as they took up their concealed positions, which made us appreciate their extraordinary ability in fieldcraft. They had remarkable eyesight and made wonderful retrievers, noting the fall of dead and wounded birds most accurately, and seldom did they return empty-handed. They spoke no English and we were dependent on Sami for communication, although it was rarely necessary as they handed over all the sandgrouse they picked. At the end we tipped them what Sami suggested, and they disappeared back into the rocky terrain with broad smiles.

I must have been placed advantageously to shoot nearly half the bag, although I had a personal reservation about an incident that occurred unexpectedly during the flight. A large pack was approaching me and, as they lost height before landing, I selected a bird on the fringe. However, as I did so they clustered together and the one I had chosen to shoot was suddenly surrounded by others. The result of this was that I was unable to avoid shooting at the covey instead of at a single bird, as young shots tend to do before they learn better. The other guns were far enough away not to have noticed what had happened and thought I had done well to achieve a total of twenty-four, not realising that half of them had resulted from one fluke shot. However, overall the flight was such an enjoyable experience that we repeated it from time to time, including 12 August 1947 when, beyond Beersheba, we had our best bag of one hundred and twenty-three sandgrouse in two hours.

Following one occasion, I recorded in my shooting notebook that 'Sami met me yesterday with the news that a friend had told him how every morning at a spot about 8 miles south of Beersheba the skies darkened with sandgrouse flighting to drink. Perhaps 50,000, perhaps more.' I had no reason to dismiss this impressive number as a wild exaggeration; I had already seen sandgrouse in clouds comparable to those of starlings in England wheeling round the sky as they gather together before coming in to roost. Unfortunately, by then our duties had increased as internal security became problematic, and none of us, so far as I know, was ever free to take advantage of such exceptional opportunities.

Before long we were facing a problem that complicated our sporting logistics throughout the next three years. This concerned the vital need to avoid running out of shotgun ammunition, and there were times when we had to make use of foreign sources, some of which were very unreliable. Fortunately, 6th Airborne Division was supported by the RAF, which operated a logistic service to and from the United Kingdom, and the Group Captain in command was happy to play his part in the cartridge supply chain. He was also keen to join in the sporting scene, with which he was less familiar, and did so spectacularly through his personal use of RAF tracer ammunition. Despite this aid, his marksmanship failed to improve, and the longer it continued the funnier it became, until the rest of us had difficulty in suppressing our laughter as his efforts, duly illuminated, were repeated on successive occasions, invariably with similar results. However, there were others, headed by our Divisional Commander, General Cassels, and the commander of the 3rd Parachute Brigade, Brigadier Lathbury, who excelled. I served on both their staffs in turn, and in each case the organisation of shooting activities became part of my duties.

General Cassels later became Chief of the Imperial General Staff and retired as a Field Marshal, while Brigadier Lathbury had further promotion to General and on retirement from the Army was appointed Governor of Gibraltar. Notwithstanding these achievements, I like to remember them both as keen sportsmen, in whose company I shot frequently with much enjoyment and minimal formality. Indeed, General Cassels was responsible for one enduring memory, because of the unusual circumstances of the occasion. He had heard of our good fortune with sandgrouse and asked me if he might come with us on our next shoot. As he was an outstanding shot and a popular commander I was delighted to welcome him, and soon afterwards the opportunity arose for him to accompany us, heading for a distant wadi that, because it had more water than its neighbours, was reported to be attracting sandgrouse for their early morning drink. Fortunately I knew it well enough to find a suitable spot to place the General in a concealed position behind a group of rocks with a fine view covering an attractive pool of water, in a healthy state following recent rain. After I had ensured he would be invisible to approaching sandgrouse I took up my own position about a hundred yards away. In due course we both had a few shots, but then the sandgrouse, instead of approaching in larger numbers as anticipated, deviated from the pool and disappeared. I was quite unable to account for this unusual behaviour, but the explanation came later from the General himself.

Following his few early shots he was surprised to see a file of Arab women, with pitchers on their heads, wending their way towards him. When they reached the pool he was overlooking, they placed their pitchers on the ground and then proceeded to divest themselves of their clothes before undertaking their ablutions. In the circumstances there was nothing he could do, least of all move and reveal his presence. In the meantime, while the Arab women took their time, with much chatter and laughter, the sandgrouse continued to be diverted and I remained in ignorance, wondering why the General, without shooting, was apparently frightening them away as they approached him. Eventually the women, ablutions completed and pitchers filled, returned to their village; but the flight which originally appeared so promising ended as a total failure. Fortunately, the General had a wonderful sense of humour, and I suspect we both dined out on his experience for many years thereafter.

Chapter 8

Recollections from Egypt and Sudan

My interest in Egyptian wildfowling was originally stimulated by H.C. Folkard, who some seventy years earlier had written *The Wildfowler*, a book that eventually became a sporting classic. In it he included a chapter headed 'Egyptian Fowling', which begins by reminding readers that, 'All classes of the ancient Egyptians delighted in the sports of the field' and mentions that this 'affords handsome remuneration to those who pursued the vocation of fowling as a means of livelihood.' Initially, the bow and arrow were used, but later more success was achieved by use of the 'throw-stick', a carefully crafted weapon that was aimed at the neck of the quarry.

It is generally accepted that the valley of the River Nile was the birthplace of ancient wildfowling and that in those times wildfowl were not only many times more numerous but also much tamer. Even so, the numbers I saw there in 1944 and 1945 were highly impressive, and among the many thousands were those that had become so used to the passing traffic that they stayed close enough to be identified from the road. The species that seemed to predominate were teal, shoveler and pintail, with mallard and ferruginous duck as minorities. But regardless of sporting considerations, I soon developed a naturalist's appreciation of the seemingly unlimited distribution of birds and animals, many of which I had not seen before. Others, like mongooses, I had seen in captivity, but here, in the wild, I was able to watch them at work hunting snakes.

Today I realise how lucky some of us were to be stationed in those parts, where the multiplicity of species, so many of which existed in abundance, was taken for granted. Moreover, we were fortunate in following several exceptional pioneers who had become authorities on the wildlife of Egypt. Among the ornithologists was Colonel R. Meinertzhagen, who published two volumes under the auspices of the Egyptian Government, then available in Cairo for 30 shillings (£1.50). At that time Egypt attracted ornithologists from several continents, and there they were confronted by such a wealth of diversity it seemed that many failed to complete the research they had intended. The opportunities facing open-minded visitors were inexhaustible; I was also interested to find that of the fifteen species of duck known in Egypt, no fewer than twelve are also recorded in the United Kingdom.

When we were encamped just south of Gaza we were less than twenty miles north of the border with Egypt and therefore had a choice of options for our sporting forays. At that time diplomatic relations between Britain and Egypt were still on the whole good, though occasionally strained; indeed, among those interested in sport, including equestrian and shooting, the friendship of former times still counted, partly due to Britain's costly defence of Egypt during the Second World War. I certainly count myself as having been fortunate to have had the opportunity to shoot duck in the Nile Delta in 1944, through the assistance of friends in the Kasr-el-Nil Barracks in Cairo who oiled the wheels for me. I had six days leave at the end of the Staff College course I had attended in Haifa and was able to go duck shooting while waiting to board the ship that would take me to Italy.

The Nile delta lies on the main route of the big annual migration of duck and snipe, so that during the winter months every stretch of marsh and wetland becomes a feeding area for the huge flights that pass southwards in the late autumn and northwards in the early spring, to join the myriads of wildfowl that dwell permanently in the delta. This great number of birds attracted both ornithologists and sportsmen from afar. The most famous duck shoot was that of the King of Egypt, but there were others almost in the same class, owned by rich Egyptian businessmen and often yielding daily bags into four figures. There were also numerous parties of enthusiasts from Alexandria who headed for the delta to enjoy the duck-shooting at weekends. The salt lake of Mariut, regarded by some as the duck paradise of Egypt, benefited from water diverted from the River Nile, and between November and February it was customarily shot on Sundays, when its 60,000 acres were shared by some fifty contributing guns. Where ownership or rights existed the privileged few would head for their personal butts with their guns and up to four hundred cartridges, occasionally returning at the end of an exhausting morning, having fired the lot. Around fifty duck per gun was regarded as an average bag during a four-hour session. The majority of those in this category of shooters were very rich men, who were accompanied by guides and pickers-up.

Transient guns, such as British Army officers visiting or passing through, would rarely have the opportunity of shooting on Lake Mariut, but a few of us had the chance to shoot within its fringes, and that was my good fortune, again while based in Southern Palestine. One of my colleagues had relations who had lived in Cairo for many years and were familiar with some of the sporting options; through them I was able to build on my previous experience, and I learned much about the duck shooting prospects on some of the extensive areas of marshland between Gaza and Alexandria that lay to the north of the road to Cairo, with which I was already familiar. Once again, therefore, I found myself as a committed wildfowler wondering why duck shooting in parts of the Middle East was so much better than anywhere known to me in Europe. Although I was not qualified to offer a scientific explanation, it seemed to me that the answer probably lay in habitat, climate and migration. However, this state of uncertainty did nothing to detract from my enjoyment of some of the best duck shooting of my life, particularly in Palestine. But it was in Egypt that for the first time I had the thrilling experience of watching a peregrine falcon dive vertically at speed to catch a duck that I had shot, before it reached the ground. I witnessed the same feat later in Palestine and in each case willingly overlooked the felony. There was, however, one important proviso of concern to all guns, which was explained to newcomers at the outset. This was the protected status of pigeons, which are sacrosanct in the eyes of all Egyptians. The taboo prohibiting the shooting of them was, so far as I know, always observed in those days.

I learned much from my visits to coastal shooting areas of Northern Egypt, and one lesson concerned the importance that was attached to decoys. Perhaps one reason for their widespread use was their minimal cost, due to cheap labour. A sackful carried by a wallad (boy), who would also set them in position and gather them at the end of a morning flight, would only cost a few piastres (at one hundred to the £). As far as I was concerned, their use contributed considerably to the prospects of good sport, and I am still using a few survivors, bought at that time, when duck shooting at home sixty-five years later. During my introduction to sport there I was often struck by the willingness to please of the fellahin (country workers), who would not hesitate to leave their jobs in order to join a shoot as beaters or game-carriers. Although they would hope for baksheesh (payment), this was by no means assured if too many of them turned up. However, they always remained cheerful, and the more intelligent ones were not slow to offer helpful advice. In fact, it seemed that the majority wished to assist and contribute towards good sport, often with a sense of humour directed at others within their group. Notwithstanding this somewhat uncertain assistance, one of my clear recollections concerns the physical effort involved for occasional guns should the necessary backup not materialise. Somehow the impedimenta required by guns in Egypt often appeared excessive.

For the benefit of English-speaking guests who were fortunate enough to be invited by an Egyptian host or managed to arrange a day's shooting, there was a small pocket guide available, written by an Englishman who had spent much of his life in Egypt. It contained a list of some forty Arabic sentences written phonetically for use when communicating with Arabs engaged as porters and retrievers. They included:

'Crouch down in the rushes.'
'Take this note to the gentleman in that butt.'
'The cartridge is stuck in the gun. Bring a long reed to push it out.'
'Mind nobody takes any cartridges.'
'Shut up, you son of sixty donkeys.'
'You idiot. Are you a shikari or a gardener?'
'Your pay is 10 piastres.'
'No more chat or I shall tell the headman.'

I doubt if any of them ever served their intended purpose, although many of us had our own selection of entertaining experiences.

Early in 1946, orders came from London to plan a major airborne exercise in the Sudan, involving outward and return flights totalling more than 2,500 miles between Khartoum and our base airfields in Southern Palestine. By then the Sudan was nearing the end of a period of more than fifty years of prosperity under the joint rule of Great Britain and Egypt, and the reception arrangements were highly organised by the host country, ending with a parachute drop by troops of the Parachute Regiment on the outskirts of Khartoum. This turned out to be somewhat hazardous owing to a sudden increase in wind velocity while the troops dropped, and there were many injuries, most of which fortunately were minor, as they landed. Nevertheless, the exercise was regarded as an impressive success.

At the time I was serving on the operations staff of the Division, and it had previously been necessary for General Cassels, the Divisional Commander, and one or two of his staff to visit Khartoum in order to assist with the arrangements. Following the completion of this task, the Governor General invited General Cassels and those of us who were with him to enjoy a cruise down the Nile in his official launch. After a luncheon ashore in keeping with the occasion, General Cassels was asked if he would care to shoot a crocodile of a size that could be put into the hands of a local taxidermist, in order to leave him with a memento from the world's longest river. The General, being the keen sportsman he was, readily accepted the offer and was duly provided with a big-game rifle for the purpose. Then, when all was ready, the guests were invited on board and we cast off.

What followed far exceeded my expectations, as the scenery changed on either bank and diverse land use and native activities claimed our attention. Here was a region that called for more time than was available to dwell on initial impressions, although the experience has remained vivid in my memory. Yet other interests closer to hand were more demanding, and our marksman's attention was riveted to the wildlife constantly passing through our line of sight. After we had reached a channel that enabled the steersman to follow a course closer to one bank, we passed a succession of crocodiles of all sizes sunning themselves on the mudbanks. One of them, estimated to be just within the suggested size limit, was selected, and within seconds the General's aim was judged to be faultless as the crocodile contorted itself before lying motionless. Then two of the crew, well armed for any emergency, waded ashore and cautiously examined the croc before attaching a rope to enable it to be lifted into the launch. All went according to plan, and in due course it was displayed on the deck for all to admire. However, before long its position was impeding the crew in their duties and it was decided to remove it into the cabin below in order to provide the necessary space on deck. My subsequent letter home completes the story:

After it had been hoisted up, the General had his photograph taken with it and then it was left in the cabin while we continued to watch the river banks go by. Half an hour later I went into the cabin to get my bathing trunks and was met by the crocodile very much alive! I have never been more nimble and beat an undignified retreat. Then we returned suitably equipped to kill it properly, but it had been quite a surprise, though the others thought it very funny!

My recollections of shooting in Egypt of course reflect my knowledge of the country and its people sixty years ago, and nowadays much is different. Although I was never stationed in those parts again I have kept in touch with friends who are aware of the changes that have taken place since the time my generation was there. Today, according to those whose work currently takes them to locations with which I was familiar, there are apparently few traces left of the natural resources that contributed to our sport. At least one attraction, however, does remain for all who have it in mind to visit that region: the sunsets I watched there were among the best I have ever seen anywhere, and intending visitors should anticipate them in the knowledge that they will enhance whatever else is sought.

An entry in my Middle East diary for 10th February 1944: 'The full moon was lovely last night and my thoughts were way back over the Solway where the Widgeon will be whistling and the Mallard quacking on the flashes.'

Chapter 9

Quail, Francolin and Chukar in Palestine

Among those who served in Palestine after the Second World War there were some, although not many, who were interested both in studying birds and in shooting those that were classed as sporting. I was one of these individuals and I look back on our operational tour, despite its blemished background of unrest and Jewish insurgency, with some satisfaction and enjoyment, not least on account of the almost limitless opportunities to widen my knowledge of the natural world while enjoying some of the best sport of a lifetime.

The quail in Palestine were those usually referred to as European quail, to distinguish them from the much larger American quail, which is also a sporting bird. My initiation into quail shooting was on 26 March 1946 and coincided with Sixth Airborne Division's first annual celebration of the Crossing of the Rhine, which was observed as a holiday by all ranks, most of whom had participated. Nevertheless, I had become aware of the arrival of quail in the fields that surrounded our camp and decided to insert a sporting break into the festivities. While these continued, I absented myself for ninety minutes, during which I flushed about a dozen quail, of which I shot six. Thus encouraged, and confident that the celebrations would continue for the remainder of the day, I decided to extend my circuit from the periphery of the camp to include a flooded wadi that led to the sea, less than half a mile distant. Before I reached it I noticed a duck among some reeds and was able to stalk and shoot this as it took to the wing, although it fell on the far side of the wadi.

As I was looking for a suitable crossing an Arab appeared, picked up the duck and, lifting the wings above its head, seemed to manipulate the bird, causing me to wonder if he had designs on it himself. However, in less than half a minute he entered the water opposite me and threw the duck fifteen or more yards, landing it at my feet. When I picked it up I saw that the wings were secured in such a way that they were locked to the body, making it a compact object to throw. Unfortunately, I failed to loosen them with sufficient care to discover how he had achieved this and I have never seen it done since. All I could do was to thank him as well as I could across the wadi.

Later in the same day I was approached by another Arab, and I asked him if he knew of any quail, using what I thought was the correct Arabic word, simmin. This he did not recognise and he shook his head, but when I indicated by sign language the bird's minute size he knew just what I meant, using the descriptive local name of firr-r-r-h. He then led me into his own field of green corn, where some quail had recently arrived, and I got half a dozen before the light began to fail and I had to hasten back to camp. This occasion was by no means unusual; indeed, I was repeatedly struck by the good nature and helpfulness of working Arab farmers, many of whom owned only a small strip of land barely large enough for the subsistence of their families. The previous day, two of us had achieved a bag of thirty quail in two hours before we ran out of cartridges, being assisted by a small party of Arab wallads who showed the enthusiasm which was always in evidence when they were on the move in pursuit of game.

A sequel to the incident of the duck thrown to me across the wadi followed soon after, when Bill Bradish, a close Irish friend, and I were shooting in the neighbouring Wadi Sukreir, where we finished inside two hours with seven species, including an unusual white-eyed pochard. The occasion was memorable and, in retrospect, amusing. One of Bill's ducks was hard-hit, although it flew on for about two hundred yards before falling. When we had picked up the other birds we had shot, and because there was nothing else to hold our attention, we decided to go in search of Bill's distant duck. Within an estimated five minutes of shooting it we arrived where it had fallen, to find three Arabs with an almost completely plucked duck and a freshly kindled fire. We reclaimed the duck, in order to show our disapproval of their intentions, but later when describing the incident we both had difficulty keeping a straight face!

Reverting to quail and the manner in which convenience seemed so often to characterise the shooting of them, 20 April 1946 provided an opportunity to combine two current pursuits as conveniently as one could wish:

Went out with a friend and combined a bathe just north of Wadi Sukreir with quailing. We stopped on the way to the beach and tried the fields along the wadi and got 4 quail. There weren't many here so we went on to bathe. After this we returned cross-country via Yibna and stopped just short of Beit Darras. Here we found quite a nice lot of birds and in 1 hour and 15 minutes shot 18, making 22 for the day.

One of the practical considerations attached to the shooting of quail was the matter of their disposal. No shooting man should command the respect of those around him if he fails to dispose properly of his bag, whatever species it may contain; if he has no responsibility for disposal he should have full confidence in those who do. In the Middle East, where many of us contributed to large bags, I was never aware of any difficulty. In a well organised unit the needs of the officers' mess would probably come first, followed by other messes, and if any birds still remained they were made available to the Arab beaters, their families and friends. However, the problem of a surplus rarely arose with quail, as they were so small that those who had shot them would expect to eat up to eight at a sitting. These smallest of game birds were quite a delicacy, and a fit gun who had been in pursuit of them would be first in line at dinner. This was in contrast to sandgrouse, which were described by Wentworth Day in *Sport in Egypt* as about 'as palatable and tender as a ball of crepe rubber'.

It is not surprising that quail ranked high in the estimation and memories of those, like myself, who regarded them as a favoured quarry. Quail spend most of their lives on the move, and the uncertainty of their whereabouts added to their sporting interest. They migrated in large numbers twice a year between Egypt and Southern Europe, mostly taking the overland route through Palestine and the Levant. It is recorded that in 1908 nearly one and a quarter million were exported from Egypt for consumption in the fashionable restaurants of Europe, although the number had dropped to less than half that after the First World War.

For those of us stationed in Palestine after the Second World War it was the informality and flexibility that contributed so much to our enjoyment of quail shooting. Even on busy days when one could not be away long from one's office, which was probably a large tent within the same camp, it was possible, by reducing mealtimes, to fit in half an hour walking up quail in the surrounding fields. We were invariably welcomed by the Arab landowners, though I was never sure if the greeting was part of their traditionally hospitable nature, or because they realised that we were likely to cause less damage walking through their crops than were the quail feeding off them. Either way, it became part of the standard procedure to be greeted by the farmers, and I found it refreshing to have even limited dialogue with these simple folk, who were leading lives that one presumed had changed little, if at all, over hundreds of years. Usually there were boys of any age hoping to be engaged as helpers. They were seldom needed to carry the game because the quail is such a diminutive bird that one can carry a large number in the pockets of most shooting garments, but they often helped in two other ways. First, their intimate knowledge of the land enabled them to point to where they knew quail were likely to be frequenting and damaging their crops, and second, through their keen eyesight they followed the flight of wounded birds and assisted in finding them.

Within our cross-section of enthusiasts was a knowledgeable ornithologist, one Captain Eric Hardy, the author of *A Handbook of the Birds of Palestine*. This remarkable guide, locally produced and unbound, lists, with comments, 364 species and a further 68 sub-species. My own copy, now over sixty years old and showing its age, soon became indispensable and remains so. Were I still linked with the same terrain it would by now have become even more important, as a means of measuring the progressive loss of natural resources in those parts. In the meantime, however, there have no doubt been other naturalists, closer to the scene, who have updated his assessment.

In consequence, species will have been identified that in some cases used to be almost ubiquitous yet have since become extinct. One example of a bird I was anxious to find, which in 1946 was not yet quite regarded as rare, was the francolin, or black partridge. As I was to discover later, however, even then this bird was in decline, and before we left Palestine at the termination of the British Mandate it had become a protected species. In the meantime it proved to be a welcome and sporting challenge, owing to its habitat in mountainous terrain and its shyness and agility in keeping out of the range of walking guns, until forced to rise by having either run out of cover or been outflanked.

Among our sporting ranks at the time were some who had recently served in India, which was an ideal posting for sportsmen. It was there that keen shots had been able to enjoy probably the best shooting of chukar available anywhere in the world; it was, therefore, an advantage to those of us who had not previously met this species to benefit from their experience when the opportunity arose. This outlook turned out to be mutual when various species were involved. Occasionally interesting differences of opinion emerged, although agreement predominated, and on no subject more so than the importance of physical fitness when negotiating rocky hills. Over a period of time it became the usual practice to apply some form of grading when planning an arduous day's sport, and the few who were clearly not fit enough were, tactfully I hope, given appropriate advice.

The chukar, sometimes referred to as the rock partridge, is a handsome hill partridge, a sub-species of the 'redleg'. At times it can be sedentary, but even so there were no easy chukars and they were virtually impossible to stalk because they blended into their background and never revealed their presence until they took to the wing. They are known to those Arabs who are familiar with them as hadjel, and as had been our experience with quail, the Arabs soon recognised our sporting interest. Moreover, even when we happened to be shooting during the harvest season, with their crops nearly ready to be brought in, they would as likely as not invite us on to their land, where boys soon joined us to beat and carry the game. As with quail, chukar might on occasions sit tight while guns walked past them, so a few boys were necessary as beaters. Sometimes it was these wallads, although presumably with the permission of their fathers, who would invite us into their fields. This was likely to be to our advantage, and by this means we got to know them and were able to be selective about which boys we employed.

As an example of the rapport we had with the Arabs, my shooting diary contains an entry for one of those days, with a team of familiar faces, which mentions a minor but unusual incident. At the end of the day, as I was paying the beaters, one boy, whom I recognised as one of the more dependable, stood to one side as the others came up for their money. After paying the rest I approached this boy with what he was due, but he waved the money away with a smile. As he did not speak any English I asked another beater, who did, why his friend had declined payment. The answer was that he had enjoyed himself so much he did not want the money, and I failed to persuade him. In case we met again I asked him for his name; thus Solomon Salim Magded went into my notebook. Although all the Arab boys were helpful and friendly, Solomon was the only beater I ever met who acted in this way.

Most of my early chukar shooting was in the Central Highlands, which comprise the hills of Samaria to the north and the Judean hills further south. Later on, I moved north with our divisional headquarters into the large monastery of Stella Maris on Mount Carmel, overlooking Haifa on the Mediterranean coast. This commanding mountain develops into a magnificent escarpment that stretches south-eastwards some twenty miles as far as the ruins of the ancient castle of Megiddo, overlooking the Plain of Esdraelon. Along the escarpment, in addition to several important historic sites, there is an isolated Druze village sprawling on both sides of a rough road running along the spine of this massive feature. Here there are commanding views across the extensive Bay of Acre to the mountains of Lebanon beyond. With good reason I recollect with awe the severity of the rocky landscape to which I was about to be introduced.

One day when I was able to escape from my office in the monastery I had the opportunity to explore this escarpment in a Jeep, and I took my shotgun with me in case I had a chance to use it. After some miles, as I approached the Druze village through which my route passed, I decided that it would be courteous to mention to one of the elders what my intentions were. Soon after entering the village I met an Arab who spoke English and asked him where I might find the Mukhtar. An introduction was soon effected, and I found him to be a friendly man, past middle age, in keeping with his responsibilities. He knew enough English to understand my greeting and wish for a brief discussion. First of all, however, came the customary invitation to partake of a cup of coffee, during which I explained what I had in mind. Before long it emerged that he, too, was a keen sporting shot, and he soon produced a somewhat antiquated shotgun. So once again I found myself in the familiar position of discussing firearms with Palestinian Arabs, whose interest in them was passionate.

In the course of our discussion it occurred to me that it might be inappropriate, if not also mannerless, to follow my original intention of going in search of chukar by myself; the Mukhtar was enthusiastic as soon as I asked him if he would like to accompany me. It turned out to be a great success, for not only did I benefit from his local knowledge but enjoyed watching his application. By now I had realised how elusive chukar were, for when compared to everything else we had shot in Palestine so far the 'rock partridge' stood by itself in the estimation of those who knew it. However, the crowning memory for me was far removed from the paltry few I managed to shoot; it was the Mukhtar who stole the show.

We made an early start, after I had returned to his village on another day, and had covered a considerable area of rough, hilly ground in the heat without seeing anything of sporting interest. As we progressed, the Mukhtar, who by now was not only directing operations but also setting the pace, had concluded that the chukar he had assured me were never far from where we stood, must be on the high ground above us. Fortunately, I was fit and keen enough to follow his plan, so we began the climb, negotiating rocks and scree on the way and eventually reaching the top of a major feature. Then, as we paused to draw breath, a covey of chukar rose just out of range and flew purposefully over the valley in front of us and onwards to a commanding hill in the distance. By then they were almost out of sight, but the Mukhtar, with his Arab's eyesight unimpaired by age, demonstrated his authority with striking conviction as he bellowed, "Look, hadjel, other-r-r mountain, QUICK". Then, with a demonstration of agility consistent with that of someone half his age, he set off down the hill we had just climbed and crossed the valley below, leaping from rock to rock with apparent ease. Nothing I saw during my time at Stella Maris impressed me more. Eventually I caught up with him, but by then the hadjel had performed their vanishing act. I returned to the monastery gameless, but with a memory to treasure.

I continued to visit the Mukhtar from time to time, partly because I always enjoyed the experience and most of the surprises he kept up his sleeve. One of these, which I suspect amused him greatly, was the day when I had been invited to sit down in Arab style to enjoy a cup of coffee. When this had been consumed he handed me a pomegranate to eat while I was still sitting cross-legged on a rug. Anyone who has eaten pomegranates will appreciate that I found it quite impossible to eat without errant seeds flying in all directions.

The Mukhtar himself was almost perfect at containing all the seeds, but never quite all. "Only Allah knows how," he explained. Within a few months I returned to England along with the rest of Sixth Airborne Division, but I always remembered the Mukhtar as one of the many Arabs I should like to have met again.

Chapter 10

Lake Hula, a Mecca for Duck

S hould the previous three chapters have exhausted my sporting memories of the Middle East it would now be fitting to move on to another part of the world. However, as the sequence of events unfolded, perhaps it was the influence of the Greek goddess Artemis, albeit with a gun and not bow and arrows, which resulted in the inclusion of a further experience that it would have been difficult to surpass. Thus, after sandgrouse, quail, francolin and chukar, all of which had their merits, the time came to enjoy the best duck shooting imaginable. This became available to sporting enthusiasts in Palestine soon after the end of the Second World War and remained so until the British Mandate ended three years later. The main venue was Lake Hula, pronounced, and often spelt, as 'Huleh'. This attractive natural feature, ten miles north of Lake Tiberias within the catchment area of the River Jordan, was overlooked in its entirety from high ground on three sides. Being some three miles long and two miles wide, it was of sufficient size to meet the needs of an exceptional range of migratory birds, as well as resident raptors.

Such was the wealth of Hula's natural resources, including a wide variety of rushes, sedges and grasses that helped to sustain millions of birds during their migration between three continents, that it would be difficult to overstate the lake's importance in biological terms, until the Israelis drained it for intensive agriculture following our withdrawal in 1948. Additionally, while it was still part of the area administered under the Mandate, the benefits to morale that a cross-section of British soldiers and Palestine Policemen derived from enjoyment of the very best sport available in the Middle East were considerable.

The Hula Shooting Club had been formed some years earlier, but had assumed a greater importance with the increase in numbers of Security Forces during the last three years of the British Mandate. The Club's affairs were conducted from Headquarters Palestine in Jerusalem, with a committee appointed and briefed by the General Officer Commanding and chaired by a principal staff officer. Members of the committee represented the Galilee District, the Services and the Police, and a permanent camp had been set up to handle the administration and the day to day organisation of parties within the five zones into which the Lake Hula area was divided. This was vitally important, to ensure that there was a fair distribution of sport and that no area was subjected to too much shooting. By mid-December 1946 the membership of the club had reached 276, and within two months it had increased to 366, although some members were only occasional participants.

To illustrate the way in which some of us were able to enjoy a weekend shooting at Hula I can reproduce part of a letter I wrote to my parents in December 1945, while I was serving with the 6th Airborne Division:

The party consisted of three of us, the other two being John Cordy Simpson, 13th/18th Hussars, who was the second in command of the Airborne Armoured Recce Regt, and another friend from the 3rd Hussars. We were well loaded up with kit, guns, ammunition and rations etc so each took a vehicle; in all two jeeps and a truck. We arranged to meet at the entrance to Sarafand Camp at 6.00 am and try and reach Tiberias (100 miles) for breakfast. This we did, going by Ramle, Lydda, Qalquilia, Tulkarm, Plain of Esdraelon, south of Nazareth, Mount Tabor and so down to Galilee. We booked in at the 'Hotel Tiberias', where I had phoned for rooms two days before, and there had breakfast. We then started off for Lake Hula, which lies to the north of Galilee. It took nearly an hour to get to Hula and we eventually arrived soon after 11.00 am. If you think of it, it's like starting from Doncaster, motoring up to Newcastle for breakfast, then up to Felton for a day's shooting, then back to N/C for dinner and the night and up to Felton again the following day at 5.30 am for the morning flight.

Well, at Hula we engaged our boats, one each, with a boatman to work it and a boy to act as retriever. We then had great fun just punting quietly round the maze of lagoons which lie on the north side of the Lake. During the two days I concentrated on duck and John Cordy Simpson on snipe. The third fellow couldn't hit a haystack and contributed 4 head to the bag in 2 days! I revelled in the duck and shot 14 and 4 snipe out of the first day's bag of 18 duck and 11 snipe. We drove back to Tiberias and had a bath and dinner, cleaned the guns and our clothes and then to bed. In the morning of the second day we got up at 4.15 and were on the lakeside as it began to get light at 5.30. The flight started soon after 6.00 and lasted a couple of hours. Then it slackened and at midday we gathered together to make plans for the afternoon. I had had a great morning with 26 ducks gathered and a number of others (about 7) lost in the reeds. In the afternoon the others went off to shoot snipe while I hid in the tall reeds along the edge of the lake. Here I shot another 22 duck and picked 16 of them. On the way back to the village I got three snipe that flew back over me very high and this completed the visit. Our bag was 110 head – 70 duck and 35 snipe and 5 various. It was the greatest fun and we all thoroughly enjoyed it. After returning to Tiberias for dinner we motored back here to Sarafand and got in at midnight.

In December 1946 Eric Bols took over from Jim Cassels as GOC 6th Airborne Division. He did not list game shooting as one of his recreations, but he in turn was succeeded by Hughie Stockwell, who was a very keen shot and was able to join us occasionally. Shortly before Christmas 1947 we had a full day at Hula, having risen at 2.15 am in order to embark at 4.00 am to get to the further shore. This involved a perilous journey for our party in two rowing boats towed by a small motor boat. The morning flight turned out to be most disappointing, but things looked up after we had paused for breakfast. I noted later that: 'The General insisted on commanding the beaters, which he did excellently. As there was a strong Westerly breeze the guns lined out at right angles to the beaters and the whole advanced Northwards with the guns in line astern, moving North and facing East. It was a great success except that we lost quite a few birds in the papyrus.' Eventually the twelve guns accounted for a bag of 110 (75 snipe, 29 teal, 2 gadwall, 1 mallard, 1 pintail, 1 stock dove and 1 quail).

Towards the end of the period in which I was regularly visiting Lake Hula the security situation, which was the reason for our presence, deteriorated and we needed to be armed and alert at all times against Jewish extremists. However, fortunately the Arabs not only remained peaceful but appeared willing to continue to contribute in several ways to our sporting activities, because with their local knowledge and water skills they had soon become indispensable to us. As can be seen from the above account, at Hula we were dependent on many who lived close enough to the lake to follow their traditional activities as fishermen and boatmen, but were also happy to be employed by us as porters, gun-loaders and 'retrievers'. In particular their eyesight, which seemed to be noticeably better than ours, enabled them not only to follow the flight of wounded birds, but to mark accurately where they landed. By this means they largely made up for our lack of dogs, which were prohibited on account of rabies. Often eager boys were better than men, and many were excellent swimmers. The keenest of them often anticipated our visits, and some developed a loyalty to individual guns which resulted in them waiting for us from one season to the next. In this regard I could not have been more fortunate, because on one of my early visits to Hula I met Abdul Latif, who turned out to be the Arab equivalent of a promising under-keeper on a well organised English shoot. At the end of that first day I asked him to provide me with his address so that I could contact him again, and thereafter he accompanied me on most of my visits during three seasons. Moreover, according to reports that I later received from friends, if duty intervened and I had to miss a weekend at Hula, Abdul made himself available to others on his own condition that he might desert them should I arrive unexpectedly! On the few occasions when he was not able to be present his place was taken by Hussein Ali Ogdi, who was less experienced but was a great character with a refreshing sense of humour. It was he who, in conversation one day, forecast "many troubles" when the British left Palestine.

One day at Hula, when Abdul's and my own attention had momentarily lapsed, I picked up one of my cartridge bags and found it lighter than it should have been. Glancing round the small group of Arabs we had engaged that day I saw there was only one strange face and I called him up in order to search him, whereupon his pockets turned out to be full of my cartridges. Our regular helpers were clearly shocked and expected to see retribution, so chastisement followed with minimal delay, using a cane plucked from the surrounding vegetation. At this the mood of the onlookers immediately changed from apprehension to hilarity at the expense of the miscreant, whose friends seemed to regard it as the entertainment of the day, laughing so much they were holding their sides. The guns then saw the funny side as well and joined in, leaving only the administrator with a straight face, though not for long.

This was subsequently regarded by some as a memorable incident in the annals of the Hula Shooting Club. The pilferage of cartridges certainly diminished, and we never had any difficulty in finding enough volunteers for any of the duties involved in a day's shooting. Wallads had an essential role as retrievers in the lake, where they performed like amphibians. While the water temperature would have been low enough to keep the guns from indulging in prolonged immersion, the Arabs we employed were content to remain concealed indefinitely semi-naked in the water among the rushes. Whenever shooting was in progress they remained fully alert and on occasions swam extensively in search of birds they had observed falling further afield.

From time to time I became aware of the friendly rivalry between our Arab pickers-up which arose from a contest of their own, related to the number of duck shot by their respective guns. This provided uncomplicated and harmonious competition until the guns unwittingly spoiled it by gathering some of their own duck. Indeed, on occasions we probably overstepped the demarcation line of what the beaters regarded as their union's responsibilities. However, time available for picking up at the end of an evening flight was limited, and occasionally we were shooting duck faster than the wallads could gather them from the papyrus and rushes. When the flight was over, therefore, guns sometimes found it necessary to join in the search as, for instance, was the case on the evening of 1 February 1948 when, according to my shooting diary, 'the best drive of the day was the last one in which the beaters drove right through the papyrus round which the guns were standing within the fringe of the lake. This had necessitated the guns walking through deep water up to chest level, with cartridge belts and bags slung round our necks, but it turned out to be well worth the effort and discomfort. Soon we were having magnificent shooting and I picked 10 duck and lost as many more in the papyrus. Later, the Arabs told us it was the first time this drive had been attempted.' At the end of that weekend our party of 10 guns had accounted for 142 head of duck and snipe.

This was the last event organised by the Hula Shooting Club in that 1947–8 season and it was certainly one of the most enjoyable. Thereafter, most members regarded their sport in Palestine as being at an end. The Club drew a line under this outstanding final season during which, in the course of fourteen weekends, the total bag had reached 6,790 head, an increase of 420 over the previous year. The breakdown was of considerable interest to those of us who liked to observe the migrational patterns among the species that contributed to our sport: mallard 248, widgeon 104, gadwall 885, pintail 77, shoveler 268, pochard 202, teal 2,561, snipe 2,245, various 100. I wrote in a letter dated 9 February 1948: 'I shall quite probably never have such a year as long as I live. My own share is approaching 500.' That has indeed proved to be the case, and how much more might it have meant to us had we realised then that we were among the last lucky few ever to shoot Lake Hula in all its natural splendour. When I flew over the same area only just over a decade later, with a party of Canadians from their National Defence College, the lake as I had known it had disappeared, the Israelis having drained it in the interests of agriculture. The extent of the consequential damage to this complex hub of birdlife and intercontinental wildfowl migration must have been considerable.

I had made a contribution to the annual Hula Shooting Club total during a particularly successful foray, for me personally, several weeks before the end of the season. In my letter home, written towards the end of January, I mentioned that during the previous weekend I had enjoyed shooting some 60 duck out of a bag of 160 to eight guns, the reason for the disparity being that the others were only occasional participants. The same letter concluded with an account of the end of the day: 'On the way back from the marsh we were attacked by Arabs armed with a variety of weapons. They almost certainly thought we were Jews. We replied with 12 bores as well as more orthodox weapons and definitely came off best. Two days earlier I had been shot at by Jews in Haifa, so you see there is rarely a dull moment!'

In writing about shooting around Lake Hula I have come across references to incidents that had faded from my memory during the intervening years, but which fortunately were mentioned in my shooting records. Friends with whom I shot enliven many recollections, and the name of John Cowtan is one of the foremost, as we served together in Palestine and shot there and elsewhere on innumerable occasions. At the end of one memorable day, when the time came to count the bag, those Arabs employed in porterage laid out the ducks shot by the guns they had assisted. It transpired that, by a remarkable coincidence, John and I had both contributed fifty, which threatened to upset the wagers between those we employed. However, it was about to become clear which gun, in their eyes, was the winner. As we assembled on the nearest bridge over the River Jordan prior to dispersal someone spotted a large fish directly beneath us. The Arabs immediately became involved in excited discussion of its merits for either the table or the camp fire, but, more importantly, how to catch it. John solved the problem by shooting vertically at the fish from the bridge, whereupon it was stunned and floated to the surface, where it was grasped by as many hands as could reach it and in no time borne in triumph out of sight, thereby enabling the River Jordan to regain its tranquillity.

Chapter 11

The Ponds of Beisan

My Palestine shooting diary entry for 20 November 1947 opens with a statement of topical interest:

Today, being the wedding of Princess Elizabeth, is a holiday throughout our forces in the Middle East.

Now, as I write this sixty-five years later with the same diary to hand, it may be relevant to mention that in those days portable radios were in their infancy and were unlikely to be found within dispersed units overseas. For this reason we were unable to listen to the commentary from London, so four of us took the opportunity to visit familiar ground in search of duck. We knew of excellent prospects within the large group of fish ponds in the Beisan area, some fifteen miles south of Lake Tiberias, and we headed for these full of hope, although the commencement of shooting was somewhat delayed. We had left Haifa at 8.00 am, but found the rough track between Samaria and Areeda so difficult to negotiate that we did not reach our destination until after 11.00 am. However, once there our hopes turned out to be well founded, and in two hours we shot twenty-four duck of seven species (teal, gadwall, mallard, pintail, ferruginous, widgeon and shoveler), together with snipe and quail.

The previous day I had asked an Auster Air OP Pilot to take me with him on a routine flight that, coincidentally, traversed the Beisan area, and this had been of value when assessing the suitability of routes within it for later use. When one is airborne it is sometimes possible, depending on visibility and altitude, not only to estimate the potential of wetlands, but also to gain an impression of their current use by wildfowl, although there were limits when it came to the identification of species from the air.

In the meantime, Christmas was approaching and our presence in the Holy Land enabled us to observe it with more meaning than we might otherwise have done. Nevertheless, a Boxing Day shoot had also been eagerly anticipated and in due course was described in my shooting diary as 'a thoroughly delightful day', although I had one or two reservations, such as, 'All the others had various excuses why they should not shoot today.' Christmas had indeed been exceedingly well celebrated by my comrades-in-arms, and the courses open to me were limited. I had arranged transport for 7.45 am and it eventually arrived at 8.45 am, after 'starting problems', or so went the driver's explanation; the previous night of festivity almost certainly had more than a little to do with it. As far as the other guns were concerned there were still none to be seen, and the moment of decision had arrived. In the circumstances I chose to wait no longer before setting out alone to visit the attractive, undeveloped area near Beisan, parts of which I already knew but now decided to explore more fully.

And so, perhaps not having indulged on the previous day quite to the extent of some of my friends, I headed off purposefully to the area I had in mind, wondering, no doubt, what might cross my path this time. On a previous occasion, in addition to duck, it had produced a jackal, which I recall as the only one I ever saw by day. This had been unusual, as it is a nocturnal creature with a mixture of characteristics found in wolves, and usually hunts in packs. Its dismal howl is familiar to country dwellers living in remote areas, but it is rarely seen by day because of its habit of secreting itself in dense cover. It is also a noteworthy predator of ground-nesting birds, including ducks, which is why this one, being careless, provided me with the opportunity to make a unique entry in my gamebook. I had surprised it sleeping in some thick rushes within the wide fringe of an expanse of water that I was surveying with a view to returning for a night duck flight. Beisan on that Boxing Day again exceeded my expectations. Because I was by myself I had been able to pursue whatever I wanted, and after six hours and a lot of walking my bag amounted to 26 head, consisting of 5 teal, 3 pintail, 1 widgeon, 1 pochard, 1 tufted duck, 1 shoveler, 1 shelduck, 1 snipe and 12 stock doves.

Shooting on Boxing Day was as much a tradition for us in Palestine as it was in the British Isles, and my shooting notebook reminds me that 26 December two years previously had been 'a really glorious day'. Gerald Lathbury, our Brigadier, and I drove from Gaza to Wadi Faliq, arriving at about 10.30 am. We then shot hard all day, because the snipe were there in numbers. By 4.00 pm we had to pause because we had used up all the cartridges in our bags. However, we had more cartridges in our vehicles and were able to refill before the duck flight that started soon after 5.00 pm, when several hundred mallard put in an appearance. We both enjoyed the day enormously and were encouraged to think that the area would be even more promising in another few weeks, because both duck and snipe seemed to be on the increase. We had both also registered the importance of having enough cartridges.

Ammunition for sporting guns was a frequent cause for concern because, as I have already mentioned, it was apt to be in short supply from time to time. I alluded to the subject in a letter I wrote to my parents in March 1946: 'The cartridge situation as far as I am concerned is looking up; the first lot of 1000 which I had sent out soon after the New Year has arrived safely [from Dickson of Edinburgh] and I have another 1500 on the way [from my gunmaker in London, W. J. Jeffery of Golden Square]. The Guards Brigade out here seem to have run short and are much concerned by the delay in replenishment.' Such was the amount of shooting we might enjoy in a day (in six weeks I fired the first thousand cartridges I had brought) we had to ensure that we did not run out, and the approved procedure was to keep spare boxes of them in a vehicle left in the care of a trustworthy Arab whose age and infirmity prevented him from filling a more active role. The security of our personal cartridge bags was our own responsibility, and most of us had a well tried system which was 'pilferage proof'; but any gun who disregarded certain basic precautions suffered the consequences. The problem arose from the fact that 12-bore cartridges had become part of the local currency system in the eyes of many Arabs, since several of them owned guns, some unsafe due to age and neglect but still used; in some areas pilferage of cartridges became endemic. When boys were caught red-handed they were sometimes given the choice of instant dismissal or 'six of the best'. But most of the Arabs we employed remained loyal and reliable, willingly accepting the very long hours and discomfort of searching extensive areas of papyrus. There was never any discussion of remuneration; they knew they would be rewarded at the end of the day, and part of the understanding was the perk of taking home to feed their families any coots that had been shot. These were either high ones shot for sport or others shot late in the day specifically for the purpose of giving to the beaters.

When I moved with 6th Airborne Division from south Palestine to north Palestine I not only kept some of my early shooting companions, but gained new ones among colleagues who had arrived from England. On 26 October 1947 a group of us had 'a most amusing day with which to start the duck season'. This was the first time we ventured to the famed Beisan fish ponds, where we eventually tried three different groups. We saw enough duck and snipe to make an interesting day, but the most remarkable feature was undoubtedly the shooting of three white-fronted geese. Seven had been spotted resting on the side of a pond, and although I did not get a shot myself, I watched with interest as two stalks took place in which the guns got within range without the slightest difficulty. The geese had probably just completed a long flight and may also have been affected by the heat, because it was a boiling hot day, well up to the reputation of the Jordan Valley.

I went back to the Beisan area at intervals when duties permitted, often with the same group of friends and particularly with John Cowtan, although he was not with us the day we invited the Navy to join us. During the first week of December 1947 HMS *Phoebe* was alongside in Haifa harbour, and five of her officers were very happy to accept our invitation to join us for a day. We took them to the ponds at Beit Alfa, a few miles west of Beisan, and got quite a bit of shooting at duck before we moved to other ponds five miles to the south-east. The final bag was not very big, possibly because the naval party had not had many opportunities for shooting, but a highlight was the lunch, a haversack meal put up by Prosses Restaurant in Haifa. Prosses was one of the best restaurants I have ever had the pleasure of patronising and would sometimes organise a 'takeaway' meal for us. I noted in my diary that on this occasion there were five varieties of sandwich and plenty of fruit.

Early in 1948 organised game shooting officially came to an end as our withdrawal from Palestine approached, although a hard core of enthusiasts, including John Cowtan, found ways of maintaining the sporting momentum by fitting in extempore days when duties permitted. On one such day I had the unusual experience of dropping a high teal directly into my cartridge bag, which was open by my side and still contained cartridges. It was inevitable, however, that as the degree of tension arising from threats to law and order increased, it had an adverse effect on sporting activities. As Jews and Arabs became progressively more jittery it became more likely that members of the security forces would become the victims of mistaken identity by one side or the other. This happened to me on several occasions while in pursuit of duck. On one occasion I had unknowingly almost reached a trip-wire connected to an explosive charge on a path between two Jewish fish ponds. Fortunately, I spotted one of those who turned out to be responsible for it running as fast as he could towards me, he having realised that I was not an Arab, for whom the booby-trap was intended. I stopped to wait for him, and it was only then that I noticed a thin, taut wire stretched across the bund, less than a foot beyond where I stood. As a member of the Security forces I was fully entitled to be where I was, and the Jews concerned had committed a serious offence. Because I was off duty on lawful recreation I did not wish to become involved in legal proceedings so did not pursue the matter, but I did not mince my words to him.

Apart from the occasion on which a party of eight of us returning from Lake Hula were attacked by a group of Arabs there was another time when three of us were heading back to camp in a Jeep in the dark one evening after a duck flight. We had just used a track to bypass an Arab village when we were fired on at close range by a trigger-happy Arab who almost certainly had mistaken us for Jews. We gave him the benefit of this doubt by instinctively returning his fire with three sub-machine guns aimed above his head, and proceeded on our way with much laughter.

It may not be expected in a sporting account of this nature to dwell unduly on other aspects of the natural world, yet such was the wealth of rare species we encountered that their presence provided a constant source of interest, so much so that my records contain many references to sightings that had filled me with awe. There were no fewer than 364 species of birds that were either indigenous to Palestine or which paused there for respite during migration, and I was fortunate enough to see many of them. I suspect that only a minority of ornithologists could distinguish at a distance between the eight varieties of falcon and, come to that, the eleven varieties of eagle. Yet somehow it was the peregrine that repeatedly caught my eye, since my awareness had been sharpened in Egypt. My diary entry for 12 November 1947 in Palestine mentions that I had paused about twenty miles south of

Haifa for a break in my duties and then, 'At dusk a Peregrine came right over me with a Teal still fluttering in its talons – a striking sight in the sunset.' And less than a month later I wrote: 'Approximately 5 miles south east of Beisan I fired at a Teal, pricking it and slowing it down although it continued on its course. Then, with faultless timing, enters the Peregrine. It came down making a noise like an express train and the Teal never knew what had hit it. The Peregrine did not cut it down, but grasped it on impact, which was loud enough for me to hear about 100 yards away.' That was the closest I have ever been to a peregrine stooping on to its prey. How could one forget such a moment!

Another particularly vivid memory is of an occasion quite early in my time in Palestine when a couple of us were walking along Wadi Rubin at 4.45 am to get into position for the morning duck flight. Suddenly the water and sky were lit by a spout of orange flame, the earth shook and the hills echoed. An ancient Arab sportsman had just fired his even more ancient weapon. He and his elderly friend were using black powder from the oldest couple of guns I ever saw outside a museum, and their brass cartridge cases I guessed were as old as the guns. We gave them all the coots we had already shot and a handful of cartridges, for which they were most grateful. In contrast to everything else about them, however, they had an excellent pointer dog, who would have held his own in any shoot.

As I write this, so many decades later, I am beset by doubts concerning the tragic events, misguided policies, oppression and intimidation that have torn apart the Palestine we knew. The last three years of the British Mandate brought many of us closer to those Arabs we had employed in the sport that we and they enjoyed so much. Whether we were in pursuit of duck, sandgrouse, quail or chukar, the keenest of us had benefited from the contribution they made in so many ways. The Arabs we knew repeatedly demonstrated how their physical senses were developed far in advance of our own, the most important of which for us was their eyesight. I often wondered if their superiority in visual detection was hereditary or the outcome of training. Whatever the answer, it was often uncanny. As a result, our bags were on average appreciably larger on the days when we were accompanied by Arabs than they would have been otherwise. Apart from this proven advantage to us, I recall with pleasure the welcome and good nature with which we were always greeted following a period of absence, and this continued at intervals until our final departure.

Sadly, this was rarely the case where the Jews were concerned, and instances of friendly relations were few and far between, even where such unpolitical activities as shooting for sport were concerned. Almost without exception, the British soldiers arriving in Palestine after the end of the Second World War were minded to be sympathetic towards the Jewish population, influenced no doubt by the treatment so many Jews had received at the hands of the Nazis. But the repeated activities of Jewish dissidents, bent on inflicting maximum casualties on the Security Forces, meant that in the course of the three years until the British Mandate ended in 1948 the Jews themselves were responsible for a complete change in outlook. However, I am glad to record a glowing exception from my diary for 13 January 1947, when I was in the Sarafand area: 'We did meet a most unusual type of Jew, a most pleasant lad who is employed as a watchman; he told me that the time to come was early in the morning and we shall try it as soon as possible.' To make such a pointed comment, however, is hardly a fitting way in which to conclude this account. Taken all round, the friends we made far outnumbered the few exceptions, while the memories of the sport we enjoyed retain their lustre undimmed and serve to balance the fact that we had not been sent to Palestine to enjoy ourselves.

Chapter 12

Turkey Hunting and Snake Catching in Georgia

W hen the British Mandate for Palestine ended in May 1948, 6th Airborne Division returned to the United Kingdom for disbandment, out of which 16th Parachute Brigade Group emerged in succession to the 1st and 6th Airborne Divisions that had contributed so much to the Allied liberation of Europe three years earlier. The 16th Parachute Brigade was commanded by Brigadier Walter Kempster, who assisted with the conversion of his units into a peacetime role. From the outset he encouraged them to become involved in as many sporting and recreational activities as time permitted. One of these activities was rifle shooting, for which he organised a brigade competition in which all units participated. At the time I was serving with 1st Parachute Battalion, the commanding officer of which was very competitively minded, and I was given the task of selecting a group of the battalion's best shots from which to form a team. This achieved the desired result during the brigade contest that followed, after which Walter Kempster arranged that I should become responsible for training a brigade team in time to compete in the next Combined Service rifle meeting at Bisley in July 1949.

During the intervening period this airborne team, which was drawn from a wide selection of corps and regiments including the Brigade of Guards, settled down well, and I still recollect the remarkable way in which its members combined their duties and recreation with such good humour; being part of it was a pleasure. It followed that when at Bisley, although they failed to appear in the prize list, they were a credit to their regiments and themselves. One veteran, who competed as usual that year, was Brigadier John Barlow, widely regarded at the time as the most experienced and successful Army competitor of that era. One day I found myself shooting next to him on the 600-yard firing point, and after we had finished, as we walked back to the club house, he questioned me about my airborne team that had impressed him with their sense of purpose and cheerfulness while, coincidentally, I had been fortunate in finishing as runner-up in the Army Championship. At the time all I knew about the brigadier, apart from his shooting prowess, was that he held an appointment in the War Office department responsible for small arms research and development.

Some weeks later, my commanding officer in the Parachute Regiment informed me that an instruction had arrived from the War Office requiring me to report for an interview concerning some future project. It turned out to have been initiated by John Barlow, who explained when I met him again that during most of the following year, 1950, a series of small arms trials would be held in the USA, involving several prototype rifles, two of which were of British design, using a new calibre of .280 inch, which was destined to supersede the .303 inch used in both World Wars. Throughout the trials a massive quantity of ammunition would be expended by fifty marksmen drawn from the US Army and the Canadian Army which for logistical reasons would represent the British Army, although a number of warrant officers from our Small Arms School would assist with supervision and statistics. In command of this small party and responsible for our interests during the trials would be the British 'user test officer'. Then came the revelation that John Barlow had nominated me for this appointment, and he hoped I would enjoy the experience.

And so, on St George's Day, which so often coincided with my changes of station or appointment, I was again on the move, this time to Washington DC for another briefing, before travelling on to Fort Benning in Georgia. While in Washington I also visited an enormous weapons research and proving establishment, which gave me a timely impression of the scale of operation to which we were committed. Then came a twenty-four-hour train journey to Fort Benning, the home of the United States Infantry, where I was to assist in a programme of trials designed to select the calibre and model of a new rifle suitable for use by the armies of the Western Alliance. It was viewed by many as the most significant undertaking of its type to date, and lasted rather over six months.

During my stay, in addition to the work schedule, there were soon opportunities to assess a vast range of country pursuits that were new to me and in the course of time increased my fund of sporting memories. Before long I was being introduced to the wildlife of Georgia and some of its many sporting options, which came about largely through the efforts of two delightful Southerners, both of whom were involved in the small arms trials. The first, Lieutenant Colonel William B. Moore, was my opposite number in the US Army and co-ordinated the programme for our joint project. The second, Corporal Carroll, was a member of the range staff, imaginatively employed in the preservation of wildlife within the vast area allocated to military training. Both men were true countrymen, motivated by an understanding and love of nature in all its moods and, as sportsmen, conscious of the need to maintain a sense of proportion when it came to their unlimited opportunities for hunting in an area comparable in size to an average English county. It was the combination of their responsibilities and a commendable attitude to a limitation of hunting that helped to ensure undue advantage was not taken of the sport available to them. In consequence, wildlife continued to flourish throughout an area that became almost a nature reserve.

When I knew Carroll well enough, I asked him if I might accompany him during some of his evening wildlife duties. This proved to be of great interest as it included my introduction to beavers, which I found quite fascinating. They are probably best known for their remarkable engineering feats, which include the ability to dam water courses, achieved by felling trees and using the timber, which they whittle with precision, before placing it exactly where required to fulfil their purpose. Carroll described this in detail through his understanding of the purpose and internal design of their 'lodges', containing living chambers, some of which would be large enough to accommodate a human lying at full length. Additionally, beavers apparently never reach the stage of accepting that they have fully achieved their objective, but energetically continue their labours indefinitely in order to keep abreast of seasonal flooding, giving rise to the expression 'working like a beaver'.

Nevertheless, when necessary, man may intervene, and Carroll was one of those who knew when and how to do so. I was fascinated not only by his own dexterity in trapping beavers but also by his understanding of where to relocate them in order to utilise their skill and industry where it would be most beneficial. Such intervention calls for much experience and judgement on the part of the human, because there are few limits to beaver ambition, or to the length of their dams, which can measure 600 metres or more. Such achievements are well within their capacity, owing to their strength, weight (up to half a hundredweight), powers of endurance and ability to remain under water for up to fifteen minutes.

Such natural wonders cannot fail to impress those who have not seen them before, but I was also privileged to be introduced to yet another fascinating wildlife activity. This time it was Bill Moore who had a card up his sleeve, and it was an ace. Lieutenant Colonel William B. Moore was an exceptionally keen sportsman and devoted to his 'bird dogs', which naturally increased our shared sporting interest; but it was the solitary pursuit of turkey hunting that he was passionate about, and he invited me to join him in this most unpredictable of sports. The wild turkey is not only unquestionably America's greatest game bird, but many knowledgeable enthusiasts claim it has no rival anywhere. It is believed that the domesticated variety travelled a full circle, being introduced into Europe from Mexico by the Spaniards in the sixteenth century, only to be taken back to North America a century or so later. The wild variety (Meleagris gallopavo) is both larger and more ornate and once was indigenous over a wide area of Northern America, being the bird that so impressed the Pilgrim Fathers. Originally so tame as to be sometimes described as stupid, it soon became so wary that it is impossible to approach, and I was given to understand that the challenge it presents was soon more than the most accomplished and experienced hunters could resist. However, even when the combination of man, weapon and fieldcraft is of the very highest standard, the turkey remains unstalkable because of its exceptional hearing and eyesight. There is a saying that a turkey can see a bumble bee doing a somersault at 400 yards. Indeed, it is only because its senses are so highly developed that it has not been hunted to extinction. It can show an impressive turn of speed when running for cover and can even fly strongly for up to a quarter of a mile.

The hunter's initial requirement, therefore, is to become sufficiently familiar with the turkey to understand its nature and ability to outwit him; and the contest that ensues is a severe test of concentration and physical endurance. There are no short cuts, but at least the sequence of events is relatively straightforward. Wild turkeys range over a wide area, so the previous day a place must be identified that they are known to be visiting to feed. Even so, one cannot be sure of one's choice, the turkey being regarded as a bird that is 'here today and gone tomorrow'. However, having located a likely place, one must then be hidden in position well before dawn and listen from the first glimmer of light for the distinctive wake-up call of 'gobble-gobble-gobble', from which the turkey gets its nickname of 'gobbler'. At this stage, the best one can hope for is to gain an impression of direction and distance, and trust that a turkey will decide to work its way towards one's hiding place. The slightest movement or sound on the part of the hunter will give the alarm. Then, as soon as one believes, from its calls, that a turkey is about to come into view, one must raise one's gun into position and hope for not too long a wait. Even in the split second it takes to pull the trigger, if the turkey has detected any movement at all it will instantly be away, and all the efforts of that morning will be wasted.

Sadly, despite all Bill Moore's enthusiasm and encouragement, no turkey ever came within distance for me to shoot and I ran out of time to make further attempts because I already had other commitments of greater importance to occupy me. Yet, even then, I felt I had made progress in the study of turkey hunting and the experience had been worthwhile. Indeed, I never abandoned the hope of accounting for a gobbler, because as well as in Georgia I had friends in both North and South Carolina and Florida, in all of which states the wild turkey is found. Meanwhile, I was presented with opportunities to participate in other activities, one of which was somewhat out of the way.

By the time I had accompanied Corporal Carroll on several evening rounds he must have felt that he knew me well enough to make an unusual suggestion. Would I care to come with him one night on a snake-hunt? At the time I must presumably have developed enough confidence in him not to find some plausible excuse to decline such an invitation, so I cautiously asked him to expand on this proposal. When he had done so I accepted his offer to accompany him, strictly as an observer. In due course we found ourselves on the edge of a large lake after dark on a still night, using a small boat just big enough to hold three of us. Carroll was the catcher, wearing thigh waders and mostly preceding the boat in shallow water, following the fringe of the lake. Strapped to his head was a lamp giving a beam bright enough to illuminate snakes without frightening too many, and in one hand he held a short rod, with a piece of strong wire fixed at right angles to its end. When blinded by the lamp most snakes hesitated, enabling Carroll to pin them with the rod before they left the water to seek cover, then, with his free hand, to catch them behind the head. The snakes thus held, he waited for the boat, paddled by a colleague, to approach so that I, no longer just an observer, could hold a bag open for every snake. As each was manoeuvred into its own bag I, as the amateur bagman, was conscious of the catcher's responsibility not to botch its descent into captivity. However, doubts were soon dispelled as cottontail vipers, night adders, rattlesnakes, brown water snakes, swamp snakes, rat snakes, cottonmouths and garter snakes were deftly dropped clear of my hands into individual bags. Thereafter Carroll disposed of them all to zoos and herpetologists.

As my time at Fort Benning came to an end I was conscious not only of the number of friends I had made in less than a year, but also of the previously unknown sporting experiences I had enjoyed. Many of them were linked with Carroll, a delightful man and an instinctive sporting naturalist, the like of whom I never met elsewhere. As an addendum I should mention that although the friends I made soon realised in what field my main sporting interests lay, there were also some who undertook to make sure I was never idle in my free time. If nothing was happening on the wildlife front at a weekend we would play three 18-hole rounds of golf on both Saturday and Sunday – the first before breakfast, the second before lunch and the last in the evening. We were all very fit.

Chapter 13

Duck Hunting in Manitoba

In 1950 the vast majority of travellers who crossed the Atlantic still did so by sea, and my first visit to North America in that year was sufficiently early in the inaugural trans-Atlantic air service provided by BOAC for all passengers to be presented with a quaintly worded decorative certificate recording the occasion. Following three introductory, pseudo-classical paragraphs, this called upon the goodwill of Phoebus Apollo, the Sun God, during the crossing and certified, in my case, that 'Major R. D. Wilson of The Parachute Regiment, having this day crossed the Atlantic in a Speedbird of BOAC, may be deemed to have well and truly 'Hopped the Pond', and I therefore pronounce him to be a fully fledged member of 'The Winged Order of Pond-Hoppers'.' It was then signed and dated by the Captain of the aircraft.

Many crossings followed in later years, and while the novelty wore off there always remained a sense of anticipation whenever there was interesting sport in prospect, none of which appealed more to me than North American duck hunting. Without doubt my own propensity for wildfowling had much to do with it, and by the time I thought that I had probably shot the last of my many Canadian ducks I felt I had qualified as a semi-resident duck hunter.

There are, of course, significant differences between North American 'waterfowl hunting' and our own wildfowling, not least in the scale of distances and numbers. During the years of which I am writing, from 1950 onwards, there were probably millions of ducks distributed in favoured areas within several million square miles between the Atlantic and Pacific oceans. Such was the appeal of this sporting prospect that duck hunting developed progressively into a major sport for a host of committed Canadian enthusiasts. They, however, belonged to a generation still untrammelled by regulations and a time when many fewer records, if any, were kept than became mandatory later. In consequence, few bags of that era were ever widely circulated; furthermore, this early generation of enthusiasts participated in a sport that prospered largely by means of an ethical code passed on within families and groups of friends, some of which developed happily into the hunting clubs of modern times.

I was detached to Canada in early October 1950. While still at Fort Benning in Georgia I had received a copy of a letter from the War Office to the Canadian Army Staff in Washington DC, explaining that the Director of Land/Air Warfare would like Major Wilson to visit the Canadian Air/ Infantry Centre at Rivers, Manitoba, in connection with the test programme for the new light automatic rifles at Fort Benning, where Canadian marksmen had been representing British interests. This request came 'demi-officially' in order to keep the Canadians informed of what was going on behind the scenes, and I was also briefed to extend my visit by a few days to make a study of Canadian Airborne tactics and training techniques.

The transit from Georgia to Manitoba involved a 2,000-mile journey, most of which was by train. As I passed through much of Tennessee, Kentucky, Indiana, Illinois, Wisconsin, Minnesota and North Dakota I gained a succession of natural and sporting impressions that Abel Chapman would have found absorbing, from the various perspectives of the sportsman, naturalist and traveller that he was. Nevertheless, both then and subsequently, it was the sheer wealth of wildfowl and the nature and extent of their habitat, coupled with their behaviour during migration, that I found so absorbing. I remembered that at one point in the journey south to Georgia the previous year I had had the good fortune to be in a train travelling in the same direction as countless thousands of waterfowl, albeit at a slightly faster speed. This aided and extended my observation to such a degree that I was able to identify at least some of the species on migration from their breeding grounds in the north to their winter ranges in the southern States; and it was not surprising in such circumstances that from time to time my mind went back to Lake Hula and the Nile Delta.

When recounting my own experience in that vast country, I am mindful of at least some of the conditions under which the enthusiasts I knew conducted their sport. This was characterised by an almost total lack of supervisory control, for the very acceptable reason that at this stage it was still unnecessary, because of the relatively modest number of sportsmen involved. Other than the need to observe close seasons, I can recall no limitations on how many duck might be shot, or where or when, in those parts of Canada which I frequented in the early 1950s.

Very soon after my arrival at the Rivers military base the subject of hunting cropped up in conversation; but notwithstanding the interest generated by all the sporting discussion and, incidentally, learning about parachuting in temperatures as low as 50 degrees Fahrenheit below zero, the primary reason for my first visit to Canada was the need to brief my hosts on the Anglo-American small arms test programme. From the outset their appreciation was much in evidence, and after a day discussing the pros and cons of the various rifles being tested, they demonstrated their hospitality by inviting me to join them on the following day in a duck hunt, with the loan of a five-shot semi-automatic 12-bore shotgun (the only time I ever had the use of such a weapon), together with ammunition, waterproofs and other necessary equipment, including decoys. It must be remembered that this was in the days before sophisticated 'breathable' waterproof materials, so getting ready for hunting meant getting kitted out in woollen underwear, thick coats and trousers and then oilskins. I recollect it as an extremely enjoyable introduction, although I only gave it a brief mention in a letter to my parents written on 9 October 1950:

> Today, being a national holiday (Canadian Thanksgiving Day), I went out duck shooting. There was a grand showing of birds – the best I have seen since Palestine, all sorts too. Met some very nice folk. It was chilly after Georgia and already they have snow and ice.

This occasion became a turning point in my experience of North American duck hunting; preparation, observation and patience, all of which must accompany it, were about to be put to the test. Thereafter, duck hunting assumed a special place among my sporting memories.

By this stage I had already seen enough Canadian wonders of nature in neighbouring duck hunting territory to be able to analyse the various aspects of alternative options. It may be that I was also learning and deriving benefit from discussing with others their outlook and practices. Many of these hunters had been familiar since boyhood with this particular annual miracle of nature as duck, in numbers beyond estimation, undertook their autumnal flight south.

The duck hunting areas to which I was taken had such numerous congregations of wildfowl they would have stirred the passion of any enthusiast. Some of the species that confronted me were unfamiliar, but I had observed enough to stimulate thoughts and questions concerning their importance in the order of merit for a wildfowler. Sometimes it seemed that the time had come for a reappraisal of priorities. I also detected a more methodical approach to the allocation of administrative tasks than I was used to when wildfowling with friends in the United Kingdom. This seemed better developed in Canada, where small groups tended to share a hut, more often than not equipped with only the basic necessities for parties of between three and five hunters.

When it came to duck recognition the first fact to assimilate was the North American practice of classifying all species of wild ducks into two groups – puddle ducks and diving ducks. The former feed either on land or in water which is shallow enough for them to reach the bottom without diving. They include mallard, gadwall, pintail, teal, shoveler and widgeon, which between them provide much of the best duck shooting in the western hemisphere. Sportsmen on the whole tend to ignore diving ducks, for two reasons; first, they often dive quicker than the time it takes to raise a gun and second, when eaten they taste fishy, with only the canvasback considered to be at all palatable. However, any diving ducks, when they fly within range of guns, are judged by the sport they offer, and culinary considerations are overlooked.

Among techniques that impressed me were the design and siting of hides, which the North Americans term 'blinds', and here they were, and I believe still may be, far ahead of us. Not only had they a range of them that was superior to ours, but they also had variations that floated and could be towed behind boats to anchor or secure in ponds, lakes, rivers and even offshore in sheltered bays. Together they provided flexibility according to the direction of the wind and other factors, by day or night.

Finally came the use of decoys, which were chosen from a range of different species and then placed, not haphazardly as can be the case elsewhere, but scientifically after due consideration. The points that had to be borne in mind were the duck species currently frequenting the area, wind conditions, local knowledge and particularly the position in relation to neighbouring blinds. As time passed and I became familiar with local practices, I began to see decoys in a different light from the few artificial ducks I had used at home. The more I saw of them in use the better I appreciated the importance of deploying them, for duck are even more perceptive than woodpigeons, which also respond to the thoughtful placing of decoys.

And so, by one means or another, I was able to enlarge my duck hunting experience. There was one occasion, with my Canadian military companions at Rivers, when there were duck migrating in their tens of thousands, flying across the full extent of our vision between two sectors of the horizon on either side of us. They were so densely bunched that we could only marvel at the sight, and perhaps it was natural that, as an occasional visitor, I could not help wondering how many noughts might follow some random numeral as an estimate of the number of duck we were observing within a given period of migration, as they passed above us in small clouds, mostly out of range.

The season of which I am writing happened to be one of the very few when almost everything went right, and these remain in the memory for the best of reasons. The 'almost' is applicable to many successful forays after wildfowl, for perfection coupled with endeavour and outcome is a rarity in any of the field sports with which I am familiar, and I would not presume to have known it more than occasionally. Nevertheless, some aspects of the sport I shared in Canada still stand out in my memory, partly due to my making new friends with shared interests. Indeed, as any experienced gun knows, there is apt to be much more to an enjoyable day's shooting than the size of the bag. On this particular splendid day at Rivers, as soon as the shooting ended there was a short pause while the guns sorted out what duck they wished to retain or dispose of, from a total that as far as I can remember was around twenty. Then it transpired that this was effectively only half-time in the activities, for clearly there was further entertainment in prospect. As events turned out, the duck shoot, enjoyable though it had been, was only the prelude to a memorable evening when shooting enthusiasts, both civil and military within and around Rivers, combined for a riotous party that continued late into the night. There is no forgetting the enthusiasm that pervaded the proceedings, and my visit to Rivers remains in my memory for the happiest of reasons. Had it not been for the thousands of miles that separate us I would have wished to return regularly to enjoy this friendship, hospitality and sport. It was stimulating to learn, since I began to write this chapter, that, although the Military Base was decommissioned in 1971, the Municipality of Daly, to which Rivers belongs, still has a reputation for excellent duck and goose hunting. Long may their traditions endure!

Chapter 14

Pheasants in Korea and Duck in Hong Kong

At the outset of the Korean War I was still in North America. Japan had annexed Korea in 1910 and the country had been divided in 1945 along the 38th Parallel, Japanese forces to the north surrendering to Soviet troops while those in the south surrendered to the Americans. By 1948 two separate republics had been declared, the Democratic Republic of Korea in the north, by then closely linked with China's regime, and the Republic of Korea in the south. On 25 June 1950 North Korea invaded across the 38th Parallel with a view to capturing the southern capital of Seoul and laying claim to the whole country. The United States army was at once mobilized for war, while the United Kingdom and the Commonwealth became involved in support of South Korea under the United Nations umbrella. We suffered heavy casualties, though it was much worse for the Koreans, who in the course of the war lost three million killed, while five million were made homeless, largely due to the scale of bombing by the United States Air Force, which dropped more bombs on Korea than it had during the Second World War.

On 11 October my regiment, the Royal Northumberland Fusiliers, sailed from Southampton, while I returned from North America to England to take up an appointment in the Ministry of Defence. Then in April 1951 came the battle of the River Imjin, in which my regiment lost 34 all ranks killed, 91 wounded and 39 taken prisoner. When it was clear that reinforcements were needed I was able to detach myself from my work in Whitehall and head for Korea, where, soon after my arrival, came the attack of 5 October on Point

217, which was my company's objective. In less than two hours nearly half the company was killed or wounded, while the rest of us expended all our ammunition and were obliged to withdraw.

While this battle was taking place our troopship was heading for Pusan to take us to Hong Kong at the end of our attachment to the Commonwealth Division in Korea. However, although the battalion's casualties had risen to 368 killed, wounded and missing, the situation remained sufficiently fluid to delay our departure, and we were placed in a reserve area until it stabilised. It was during this hiatus, when we were out of the battle line, that we were able to indulge in some sporting recreation, having handed over to 1st Battalion Royal Leicestershire Regiment on 18 October. Charles Mitchell, despite having been seriously wounded during the Imjin battle, had still found it possible to send me a signal before I left the United Kingdom, advising me to bring a shotgun and plenty of cartridges.

When the time eventually came for us to be reunited with our shotguns, which had been stowed in a three-ton truck in the battalion's administrative echelon, there were as yet no opportunities to arrange any co-ordinated sport for shooting parties; yet it was surprising to find how conditions favoured one or two guns with a handful of beaters forcing their way through rough semi-jungle. Happily I already had four experienced and keen Northumbrian volunteers in my own company, who in no time had taken up the challenge of acting as beaters as if they had grown up with it, and certainly there was no shortage of enthusiasm. On reflection I concluded that it was a combination of complete contrast to their preoccupation with recent events on active service and the prospect of good sport that stimulated everyone in mind and body, as a letter to my parents dated 20 October suggested:

Am now going to break off while I go out to chase some pheasants which I know of – have had 22 so far since we came out of the line, all walking up. Last week 2 old cocks ran ahead so far and fast that they found themselves on the edge of a Korean village, whereupon they decided that they were far enough from their own haunts and broke back. By the time they passed over me they were flying high and fast, but I managed to get them both. For one glorious moment I was back in England and never pleased myself more.

Then, on 22 October I added:

I have been meaning to get this finished and sent off. Since I started it I have had two more days (or rather, a few more hours) shooting. The first time was one afternoon by myself with 4 beaters when I got 10 pheasants; the second occasion was yesterday when I went out with 2 other guns and the same 4 beaters (walking up each time) and we got 5 between us. How often we misjudge prospects; sometimes when walking up I might expect to finish with a larger bag by myself than when in company with one or two others. It is partly a matter of not wasting time while trying to share the shooting, and, most important, a lack of flexibility. When you are by yourself you go where you please and change direction as the need arises, in order to cover the most likely areas. In other words, by thinking as a pheasant might, you often find them more easily and anticipate their line of flight. With a line of walking guns you decide on the beat and then cover it without deviation. However, on reflection I believe 2 guns can be the best combination when seeking the best sport while rough shooting.

That was my view sixty years ago, and although I added my opinion that the redoubtable Colonel Peter Hawker (1802-1853) would probably have pronounced that two guns are one too many, I later came to the conclusion that three guns when rough shooting can still be a very attractive combination. Today there are several reasons why two or three walking guns are seldom seen in many parts of England: one is because of the diminishing extent of available shooting terrain, due to urban sprawl and intensive agriculture; another is the preference for driven game which is allied to the expansion of commercial shoots. Happily, in Korea the only restriction was apt to be our understandable preoccupation with the war. My record made at the time includes the impression that it was highly unlikely the land which we walked up with our few beaters had ever previously heard the report of a shotgun, although it had reverberated to the various sounds of distant battle.

One of the relatively few convivial memories of my service in Korea was the renewal of our joint interest in sport that I had shared with General Cassels when he was commanding 6th Airborne Division in Palestine. Six years later he was commanding the 1st Commonwealth Division in Korea, which included the Royal Northumberland Fusiliers, and he had been instrumental in ensuring that I reached them when I was in danger of being diverted elsewhere. When the time came for my regiment to leave Korea I felt the least I could do to show my appreciation would be to give him a brace of pheasants. Unfortunately, he was out of his headquarters when I arrived there, so I left the birds with a note of thanks. The following day, as we were about to join the transport that would take us to catch our ship at Pusan I received the following letter, which illustrated both his keenness and his marksmanship:

> Thank you very much for the pheasants which are most welcome. It was very kind of you to send them. Just after your present arrived I saw an old cock land by the CRA's caravan. I leapt to a gun, flushed him and dropped him by the mess kitchen alongside yours! – all very tidy ... Yours ever, Jim C

I saw much more of him during the following years, up to and beyond his retirement as one of the last Field Marshals in the British Army. Occasionally I met him in London, where even affairs of state and many of the problems associated with them failed to deprive him of his sporting interests. Later still, in Scotland following his retirement, we would meet from time to time and discuss, as sportsmen do, our relative sporting activities. Today, I suspect, the ancient tradition of British Army officers combining sport with soldiering on active service belongs to the past, due largely to the increased tempo of modern warfare. On the other hand, perhaps the 11/- (55p) a day we were paid when 2nd Lieutenants should not be overlooked.

In Korea, as elsewhere on active service, the spoils of our game shooting were a welcome supplement to the daily rations. At the time we had little information concerning the birds confronting us; all we had been told was that there were some indigenous pheasants in Korea. I personally had no prior knowledge about them at all, and it was fascinating gradually to gather some facts. As time passed we learned considerably more from our own observations than from other sources, which were by no means consistent. For example, the Korean ring-necked pheasant is referred to by one authority as Phasianus colchicus karpowi and by another as Pasianus colchicus pallasi; both of these have a resemblance to the strain best known in the United Kingdom except in size, which in both Korean cases is larger. From my own observations the colouration was consistent with that of the average English cock pheasant,

The end of a hunt with the Braes of Derwent, c.1925. The author on 'Mousie' with his sister on 'Sammy'. (From the *Newcastle Chronicle*)

'The Venture' coach driven by the author's grandfather George Burgess, crossing the Northumbrian Derwent near Edmonbyers, 1934.

Preparing to set off from Eddy's Bridge on the Northumbrian Derwent, September 1934.

The best of a day's catch as a teenager on the River Coquet, 1936.

A good morning's sport as a septuagenarian on the Aberdeenshire Dee, May 1994.

Wildfowling on the Solway with Dinah, November 1941. A break from instructional duties at Annan.

Preparing for reconnaissance with Peggy, a Lakeland terrier, when Chief Instructor, 3rd Division Battle School, Moffat, Dumfriesshire, autumn 1943.

Charles Mitchell with his guests, 'fell in ready for the off' above Ardeonaig, August 1956.

Charles discussing prospects with the author's Labrador Duchess, before grouse shooting on his moor in Perthshire, August 1956.

In anticipation of grouse on the Dirnanean moor in Perthshire, with Dora in attendance, August 1974.

An unlucky impala, shot earlier that day, being prepared as a welcome supplement to soldiers' rations, Kenya, 1953.

A bag of guineafowl, with RNF volunteer beaters, Kenya, 1953.

Royal Northumberland Fusiliers enjoying a camp fire meal while on safari in the Kenyan bush.

Arriving from camp near Brunswick for a duck flight; with portable hide loaded on the jeep, Germany, 1949.

A colleague wading ashore after duck shooting near Brunswick, Germany, during the post-war occupation, 1949.

REGULAR ARMY U.S. VIII - BISLEY, 1949

Back Row: R.S.M. A. G. Pettit, R.E.M.E.   Major R. M. Parsons, R.U.R.   Cpl. J. Gillam, South Lancs. Regt.   E.Q.M.S. H. Malpas, E.E. Pendine.

Front Row: Major R. D. Wilson, Parachute Regt.   Capt. W. H. Baudains, R.U.R.   Brig. J. A. Barlow, C.B.E.   Capt. J. W. Moore, Bedfs. & Herts. Regt.
E.Q.M.S. F. Herbert, E.E. Pendine.   E.S.M. A. Martin, E.E. Pendine.

Sitting: Capt. V. H. Viney, R.E.M.E. *(Reserve).*

Regular Army shooting VIII in United Services contest, Bisley, 1949.

The author preparing to start from 'Top' on the Cresta Run, 1958.

The Services Cresta teams of 1958. From the right: Royal Navy, Army (winners), RAF. The author back row fourth from right.

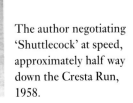

The author negotiating 'Shuttlecock' at speed, approximately half way down the Cresta Run, 1958.

The author with rival parachute
team captain (Canada), looking
relaxed after competition,
Hereford racecourse, July 1962.

SEP · 62

The author with rival parachute team captain
(USA), subsequently a firm friend, looking pensive
before competing in the Adriatic Cup, Portoroz,
Yugoslavia, August 1963.

Aerial view of the World Para-Ski Race, Vermont,
16 March 1963. The target was the small cross in
the widening at the top of the run. The straight
ascent to the summit is the route of the cable car.

SAS Free Fall Parachute Team during pre-flight briefing before the jump from 34,350 feet, Boscombe Down, 30 January 1962. The author on the right.

The team ready to emplane before the jump, which set a new British altitude record.

The author dressed and equipped as a US major for a standard parachute jump in order to compare British and American procedures, Fort Benning, Georgia, 1950.

The author after exit from aircraft over Orange, Massachusetts (photo by Joe Gonzales, US Army Parachute Team photographer), August 1962.

Alexander (aged two and a half) showing an early interest in pheasant rearing, August 1982.

Sheep dipping on the farm – not just a spectator sport. The author supervised by his family, 1984.

Peter (aged five and a half) preparing to accompany a field marshal, six generals and a doctor on the 'Generals' Day', 21 November 1987.

Dinah in the early 1940s. The
first of the line and life-saver
in a blizzard.

Dimple in the late 1960s.
Mistress of all she surveys.

Diamond waiting for master to return
by parachute, 1961.

Peter's first grilse, hooked and played in the Trolley Pool on the River Nith and netted by Alexander, July 1991.

The Glorious Twelfth in Inverness-shire, 1995. Alexander's and Peter's first day's grouse shooting.

Combeland in February 1965, accessible only by foot or on horseback.

Collapsed walls after the rafters had been removed, April 1965.

Ready for occupation, August 1966.

Combeland after nearly fifty years in residence.

Aerial view at the start of the salmon fishing season. The Meeting of the Waters, where the Little Exe joins the Barle to become the River Exe, with the renowned Black Pool downstream.

'A Regimental Day', December 1982 (painting by Denise Bates). The Fifth Fusiliers are identified by the V of larch in the plantation behind the house.

although it is recognised that even here there are slight variations among 'ring-necks'. Where the main difference lies, and it is most striking, is in the size/weight factor, which is sufficiently obvious to dispel all doubt. The Korean pheasant is on average at least one and a half times the weight of its British counterpart. A cruder, but practical, comparison that I was able to draw was based on the average British soldier's appetite. 'In the field' two hungry soldiers would leave very little from an English cock pheasant, whereas a Korean cock would be quite enough for three.

What we lacked most in Korea, of course, were dogs, and I never saw one there trained to retrieve. This was a pity, because many birds were lost, as well as time wasted, for the lack of them. As it was we failed to find even more birds than we might have expected in dense cover and declivities within the rocky areas. However, there were also cultivated paddy fields that were not only more easily traversed, but sometimes held far more pheasants than we found elsewhere, and the villagers were happy for us to scare them away. My overall impression therefore, which helps to put the bloody side of our Korean sojourn into perspective, is that without our recreational sport our time in that theatre of war would have been memorable only for all the worst reasons.

Following departure from Pusan after our tour of active service in Korea my regiment sailed for Hong Kong, where we were to spend a further year of mixed fortunes in the Far East, at the northern end of the New Territories, which cover some 355 square miles of mainland north of Hong Kong island. Here we had a defensive role related to the possible threat of an incursion by the Republic of China; notwithstanding existing treaties between our two countries, we were required to establish part of a screen of small outposts to provide early warning of such an eventuality. We were based about a mile from the border and, being well separated by 26 miles of rough road from the Island's bright lights, most of us were limited to visits there at intervals of several weeks, partly due to restrictions on the use of recreational transport. Our initial assessment of the weather in late October as being pleasant, with hot sun by day and agreeably cool nights, was over-optimistic; but life in camp was made as tolerable as a mosquito-infested, swampy area, in humid, sub-tropical conditions with periodic monsoon rains permitted. Our basic, though not altogether Spartan, abode, incongruously named Norwegian Farm Camp, lay about a mile and a half from the sea and less than 100 feet above sea level;

and in the eyes of the vast majority of its occupants it was sadly wanting in desirable facilities, especially as the sea was deemed unfit for bathing. Therefore, whether for operational reasons or as a means of keeping some 650 soldiers occupied, we were tasked on five days each week to dig trenches across the full extent of two mountainous features known as Hadden Hill and Snowdon. These overlooked the camp from north and south respectively, at approximately 1,000 feet above sea level.

The digging of a lengthy trench system, however, only amounted to Phase 1; it was followed by Phase 2, which involved constructing successive belts of wire obstacles, the defence stores for which included an impressive tonnage of barbed-wire rolls and angle-iron pickets. Moreover, so steep and rocky was the ground that no vehicles or mechanical equipment could be used and, as no coolie labour or mules had been brought in to assist, all the materials had to be carried by hand. In consequence, the whole project became one of hard labour by British troops that must have matched, if not exceeded, that of many penal establishments within the Empire. Not surprisingly, in the hot and humid climate, and before most of us had seen an air conditioning plant, many were soon suffering from skin complaints, and the daily sick parade rose to a level that came as a surprise, even to our Royal Army Medical Corps staff.

This, incidentally, was the only time I can recall during my military service in which company officers, of their own volition, felt the need to strip to the waist and spend the day alongside their fusiliers, working manually to a plan that was sufficiently clear-cut to require minimal supervision. Within Z Company my sergeant major was still recovering from Korean War wounds, but was able to act as foreman of an all-ranks labour gang. While there was no suggestion of mirth in evidence, this nevertheless assisted morale at a time when many of us were feeling critical of an apparent lack of judgement at a higher level. Nevertheless, our Geordie soldiers accepted the situation, as was their wont, particularly when assisted by the timely arrival of a consignment of Newcastle Brown and Amber Ales which, in such circumstances, had a magical effect.

During the lulls between military activities, I had been familiarising myself with that part of the coastline nearest our camp. Although the response to any enquiry about whether there was any game to shoot in the area was always negative, I was determined to satisfy myself that this was really so, because it seemed to me to have many of the attributes sought by wildfowl. One evening a couple of weeks after we had settled into our camp, I took a stroll down to the marsh at dusk. There was plenty of fresh water close by, used for irrigation of the paddy fields and watercress beds that were under intense management, and as I surveyed the scene I became aware of a constant movement of wildfowl, which flew in and out of the crops without heeding any of the people at work. The only conclusion I could draw was that they were never shot at, and I wondered whether it was because the duck were protected or because neither the coolies nor their employers owned a shotgun. There was no way, at that time, of finding the answer, and I guessed that this was neither the place nor the occasion to use a gun. However, I returned to camp and consulted an excellent map – the same one that I have now before me as I write – Hong Kong and the New Territories North Sheet, Scale 1:80,000, published by the War Office in 1936. To the west of where I had been standing lay Hau Hoi Wan, under which appeared 'Deep Bay'. No keen wildfowler could even glance at it without a surge of interest, because it was so consistent in character with so many estuaries in the British Isles which have a sporting reputation. This area of foreshore was without cultivation and there appeared to be no restrictions on anyone wishing to make use of a shotgun so, as soon as conditions appeared favourable, I went on an evening flight. On that first occasion I saw altogether 70 – 80 duck and dropped two, though I failed to pick either as they fell into bog. However, through the winter I was able to repeat the process and would return to camp with a number of duck for later consumption. As an aside, it is interesting to remember that while we were able to supplement our basic rations with local produce we were also in the habit of sending food parcels to our families at home, still under the restrictions of rationing. The birds I shot were all ones with which I was familiar, such as mallard and tufted duck, although I did occasionally see rarer varieties not found in Europe.

After a while I felt I wanted a dog, so rang up a kennels I had seen advertised and found that they had a two-year-old bitch Labrador. When I went to meet her she appeared very friendly and persuaded me to overlook her shortcoming of being yellow. As I knew I would have no trouble in finding a good home for her when it was time for me to leave Hong Kong, I bought her and a couple of weeks later wrote home that she, Lady, was turning out to be quite a character. She became more of a pet every day, and although initially I almost despaired of her becoming a gundog, because she seemed to have no interest in retrieving, eventually she began to realise what was expected of her. At the end of our tour I left her with a family who regarded her as a pet as well as a working dog, and during the long voyage back to England I was able to look forward to the welcome I knew I would receive from my own black Labrador at home.

Chapter 15

White-fronted Geese in Wexford

During the 1952-3 shooting season I had the memorable experience of an extended week's wildfowling in the south of Ireland. It differed in some respects from the wildfowling I was familiar with in England and Scotland, principally because I was a guest in an organised shooting party rather than following solitary sport. My visit was made possible by my delightful and effervescent Irish friend, Bill Bradish, whom I had first met seven years earlier when we became close associates while serving with 6th Airborne Division in Palestine. He has already made an appearance in my account of game shooting there, the day at Wadi Sukreir when he and I accounted for seven different species in two hours. We shot together on many occasions and shared some wonderful sport with mutual friends at Lake Hula and also at Wadi Faliq, though Bill missed the latter on Boxing Day 1945 due to a nasty road accident in which he had been involved on Christmas Day. In his absence our brigade commander, Gerald Lathbury, and I shared the irritation of running out of cartridges in the course of shooting 14 duck and 41 snipe in the same wadi. But Hula remained the shooting Mecca for all of us.

In June 1951, while I was working in Whitehall, I received what I regarded as an irresistible shooting invitation from Bill Bradish, writing from his home in County Wexford in his usual entertaining style:

Firstly, we shall be <u>delighted</u> to see you and Duchess [offspring of Dinah] for the first week in November. We are assaulting the duck and

geese on Saturday 3rd November and it's <u>essential</u> that you are there for
that day as the geese will be fresh in and some of them still comparatively
uneducated!

There followed detailed travel guidance, somewhat similar to that given to a
prep school boy due to return home by train unaccompanied at the end of his
first term:

> Boats arrive at Rosslare from Fishguard on Tuesdays, Thursdays and
> Saturdays early in the morning and therefore you must arrive <u>at the</u>
> <u>latest</u> by the boat which gets here early on the morning of Thursday 1st
> November, since the next boat would be too late. This will mean you
> leaving Paddington on the 6.55 pm on Wednesday 31st Oct. Drop me a
> line as soon as you can to say if this is OK. Stay as long as you like – the
> longer the better.

The shooting in prospect was to be on the North Slobs, polderland drained
for farming on the northern side of the River Slaney's estuary. This invitation
had been particularly attractive to me because it was an antidote to the tedium,
for a countryman, of living and working in London. However, as it happened,
the tedium was to be relieved in a rather different way: within weeks of
receiving Bill's letter I had been released from the Whitehall appointment
and by the end of July had set sail from Liverpool on HMT *Devonshire*,
bound for Korea. My interval in the Far East lasted just over a year, and on
25 August 1952 I was once again in Liverpool, disembarking from the *Empire*
Pride after a voyage with my regiment from Hong Kong. I must have let Bill
Bradish know that I was on my way back to England, because he lost no time
in getting in touch, and when I got home I found a letter sent from Wexford
on 24 August: 'How splendid to hear from you again and even better to hear
so comparatively quickly. I had feared that we might have seen the last of you
for several years.' There followed some expressions of professional interest
in what we had experienced in Korea, before the letter reverted to its really
important subject:

> Our invitation for you to come over here and stay with us is more than
> open and the sooner plans are made the better. Our geese <u>normally</u> arrive

about mid-October and are with us from then till the end of the season (<u>end</u> of Feb here!) Any time that fits in with your plans will suit us, but if asked to pick a good all round period, including snipe, I think I would choose the end of November and beginning of December. That is a very dangerous thing to have said since, as you will well know, we are <u>entirely</u> dependent on the weather. As soon as leave plans start to get made let me know what the form is and I will lay things on at this end. Duchess is <u>more</u> than welcome too.

Last season's shooting was fair on the whole and personally I had a super year, mostly due to luck. I always seemed to be surrounded by birds even on the most hopelessly calm and sunny days. My last bag on the Slob was a 54, consisting of 11 Widgeon, 8 Geese, 27 Golden Plover, 3 Teal, 2 Pintail and 3 Tufted Duck shot in the most unlikely conditions. Best bag of geese to my own gun on any day was 21 (all White-fronts except for 1 Greylag which should have been a lot higher). Total geese for the season was 83. There was a fair showing of snipe but they seemed very unsettled all the season. We had an outstanding day when 2 guns and self collected 52, and on a later occasion, when accompanied by two blind fools, who shot nothing, I saw more snipe in one day than I have ever seen here before.

Bill explained that the duck and goose shooting rights on the area known as the Slob were owned by his uncle, Joshua Nunn, who needed plenty of notice so that I could be fitted into his plans, which were always made well in advance: 'It will be grand to see you again and the earlier you can give me even forecast dates the easier it will be to get some sport organised.' As I was giving immediate thought to this invitation the Army intervened with its own ideas, linked with the Cold War, which ruled out all foreign leave until after Christmas, thereby also causing much disappointment among early season winter sports enthusiasts. However, the Bradish and Nunn families were familiar with such eventualities, and Bill soon came up with an alternative invitation for me to arrive on Boxing Day, which raised no problems for me. In the meantime we remained in close touch, and periodic bulletins from Bill kept me informed of wildfowling news and prospects, often humorously:

Had an amusing incident on the last shoot. Was 'looking after' a rather nice old man who has been reduced by age to shooting with a 20 bore. Six White-fronted approached us pretty lowish and we both got a right and left. The survivors were so amazed that they returned to see what had happened, and we each fixed one of them – total 6 geese in 30 seconds!! NOT likely to be repeated in the near future!

If Bill were still alive I wonder how he would regard me today, shooting in my nineties with my 20 bore, if he had not already found his own 12 bore too heavy and made the same conversion. However, back in 1952 Bill continued to write with shooting updates and necessary information:

I am enclosing all the dope about getting your guns etc into this wild land so that you can get weaving without delay … I suggest you start making bookings pretty soon now – particularly your sailing ticket for night 26/27 Dec … You will want a cabin on the boat and you can obtain one by writing to the Harbour and Quay Superintendent (Cabin Reservations), British Railways Western Region, Fishguard Harbour, South Wales and enclosing the sum of 12/6 [62½p] … I think that we are now all clear for foot and mouth, but you should make pretty certain before you set out or poor old Duchess may well find herself refused entry, which would be most awkward!

P.S. Normal filthy shooting clothes, a suit and a dinner jacket is all that is needed. NO pansy stuff!!

And so my long awaited visit to Ireland finally came about, and I arrived in Wexford after spending Christmas with my parents on the edge of Exmoor. I had managed to extend my leave and was able to enjoy eight days' shooting, the sequence of which was only broken by an intervening Sunday. Remarkably, every day was spent on a different beat, each of which had its own merits and characteristics, so for me it developed into a unique and memorable sporting holiday. I had the additional interest of having brought with me, as well as my usual game gun, a recently acquired 12 bore magnum suitable for 3-inch cartridges with heavier loads. It took me a day or two to get used to it, during which I shot indifferently, but soon, with practice, my performance improved, and I came to appreciate its many advantages.

As this wonderful shooting experience progressed I formed the impression that much about it was in a class of its own, and that is still my opinion. An early highlight occurred on my first day when I was confronted by the first white-fronted geese I had ever knowingly seen. Until then my wildfowling experience had included greylag, pink-footed, bean, barnacle, brent and Canada geese, but here was a missing species with numerous interesting characteristics. Among these, from a wildfowler's standpoint, is its ability, when alarmed, to rise at speed almost vertically from the ground, which can be quite a challenge for those unfamiliar with it. So, with this exceptional background and the constant presence or promise of geese, all enhanced by my competent and entertaining host, the prospects could not have been more inviting. Only the weather, which was insufficiently rough for the best wildfowling, was neutral in the presence of man and goose.

Apart from this limited reservation, however, the holiday came as close to perfection as even the most ardent wildfowler could wish; from my own standpoint, any day's wildfowling ending with a personal bag of geese in double figures has to be a memorable experience. Happily it was shared on this occasion by Duchess who, as so often, made her own contribution. By this time Bill had seen enough of her to recognise her qualities as a gundog, but following the last drive of the day she gained further admirers, as my game book records:

The day ended with a brilliant retrieve by Duchess across a small river for a teal shot earlier by another gun. She crossed the river three times and eventually found it with a damaged wing some way from where it fell. This, I felt sure, helped to make her day, as it did also for me.

Among her many admirers, Bill Bradish's wife Bridget, known as Bids, must have been high on Duchess's list. Each day, following her return to our host's house, I would dry and feed Duchess, after which she was allowed to join us in front of a splendid fire. Then, as bedtime approached, she was permitted by Bids to accompany me upstairs to my bedroom, where she slept soundly on a blanket in a large clothes cupboard. She made such an impression that Bids still remembered this vividly sixty years later, and when reminded of it

I was able to picture it too. I am also of the opinion that her current direct descendant would have behaved in exactly the same way and been just as popular in similar circumstances.

As the date of my departure approached I realised there were several aspects of this memorable holiday that I had found refreshing, one of which predominated. It was the carefree atmosphere, coupled with a sense of commitment to ensure that everyone, whether guest or host, would enjoy him or herself to the utmost. The Nunn and Bradish families shone consistently in providing a subtle blend of sound management and nature conservation, with Irish lightheartedness accompanying the proceedings throughout.

My opinion of wildfowling in Ireland in the early 1950s is put in perspective by the account in The New Wildfowler of the 1970s, with a preface by Peter Scott which contains the following passage:

Pinkfeet are rare in Ireland, and the Bean goose is uncommon; by contrast Greylags winter in the west of Ireland and in Counties Down and Wexford, but in decreasing numbers. The shooting on the Wexford Slobs, or marshes, is in private hands and carefully controlled; as a result, the goose shooting on the Slobs probably surpasses anything else of its kind in the British Isles. Some winters odd specimens of snow geese turn up with the Whitefronts on the Wexford Slobs.

When I was going through my letters and shooting records to fill in some gaps I was absolutely delighted to find that Bill Bradish's son Patrick is still living in the house I remember so well. The shooting rights formerly held by the Nunn family are now in different hands, and the North Slob is now part of Wexford Nature Reserve. When I contacted Patrick he was able to put me in touch with Dominic Berridge, the Warden of the Reserve, whose father coincidentally had been serving in Palestine at the same time as Bill and me. I had been aware that the Wexford Slobs are internationally famous as a winter haven for wild geese, the earliest reported sightings being of greylags in the late nineteenth century, arriving from their breeding grounds in Iceland. Gradually the white-fronted geese appeared from about 1910, building up to several thousand by the mid-1930s and almost entirely replacing the greylags.

My memories of the Slobs in the middle of the last century are so vivid that I found myself wanting to know how they are faring nowadays, and Dominic Berridge became a splendidly helpful source of information, including a resumé sent by email, perhaps the modern equivalent of Bill Bradish's entertaining handwritten letters:

The nature reserve started in the late 1960s when a parcel of land was acquired at the west end of the Slob near the pump house. It was bought in partnership between the Department of Lands (who then ran the National Parks and Wildlife Service) and what was at that time called the Irish Wildbird Conservancy (now called BirdWatch Ireland and a sister organization to the Royal Society for the Protection of Birds). Guinness put up some of the money. Two or three further contiguous parcels have been added since then. Nowadays day-to-day running is done by the National Parks and Wildlife Service.

The main aim of the reserve is to conserve the Greenland White-fronted Geese which took to wintering here in greater and greater numbers as their natural habitats in the midlands and west were damaged by bog exploitation for peat (always called turf in Ireland), which accelerated during and after the war. There are also over 20,000 other waterfowl in the Slobs/Harbour/Lower Slaney area, which means that it qualifies under the EU Birds Directive as a 'Special Protection Area'. This allows certain grant aid to farmers paid for actions carried out under an agreed farm plan. The reserve is let to North Slob farmers for the summer for nominal rent; they graze it and take hay etc off, then leave for the winter and part of the deal is that they put up with goose grazing on their Slob fields until April.

Now the Slob holds one third (c. 8,000) of the Greenland race. These geese, nearly alone among grey geese, are in decline, perhaps due to complex climatic reasons in Greenland and Iceland. So shooting them has been banned. The four syndicates on the Slob shoot mallard, teal, widgeon, tufted, pochard, golden plover, snipe and pheasant etc.

That's it in a nutshell.

It is sad to learn that the white-fronts wintering in Wexford are in decline, but reassuring to know that steps are being taken to conserve them. For my own part, the knowledge that their numbers are currently reduced casts no shadow over my memories of the shared pleasure of a wildfowling holiday, for in those days the geese were coming in ever increasing numbers and farmers were given no recompense for the damage they caused to the grazing each winter. As in so many situations, it is the balance of nature that we must strive to maintain.

Chapter 16

Sporting Options in Kenya

It was during the late summer of 1953, following the Queen's Coronation, that I accompanied my regiment to Kenya. We travelled by air, which in those days was a novelty, following centuries of trooping by sea, and made our way some 120 miles north of Nairobi airport to reassemble under canvas in an area around the settlement of Ol Joro Orok. This was near Thomson's Falls in the Northern Aberdares, where we were overlooked by Mount Kenya, a formidable feature of 17,058 feet with a challenging summit. It had been established as a Royal National Park only four years earlier and well did it deserve this status, supporting then no less than 40 species of mammals and 128 species of birds.

However, it was neither the terrain nor the wealth of wildlife that claimed our primary attention, for we had been sent to Kenya with the clear-cut operational purpose of assisting in the suppression of the Mau Mau rebellion, which had erupted with much violence and loss of life the previous year. We, the Royal Northumberland Fusiliers, took over from the Devonshire Regiment, who had established an enviable reputation for fieldcraft. Our priority at the outset, therefore, was for all ranks to reach the necessary level of physical fitness to achieve anything liable to be required of them. On arrival we were faced with the immediate need of coming to terms with breathlessness, caused by the 10,000 feet height above sea level of our camp. Such had been the intensity of the preparations for our move from the United Kingdom, coupled perhaps with the odd lapse in pre-departure briefing, that the effects of strenuous physical effort on arrival at such an altitude had been, at least partially, overlooked. Thus breaking into a double in order to give more time at the far end failed to achieve its purpose, and buglers sounding routine calls ran out of puff and were apt to fail to complete their task. In these circumstances an important attribute was a sense of humour, although this was tested soon after our arrival when it emerged, to the dismay of our Geordie soldiers, that there appeared to be no pub, or equivalent, in the settlement of our adoption. "Not even in our hemisphere", observed the company clerk darkly, after he had noted that the equator passed between our camp and the nearest public bar down the road, which turned out to be the 'Sportsman's Arms'.

It had been well before this stage, and possibly as early as when the first mention of Kenya began to circulate back in Barnard Castle, that forest sports became contenders among personal planning priorities, at least for an enthusiastic minority, of which I was one. Indeed, the experience gained from sport in Palestine five years earlier came to the fore, with the additional prospect of fishing, which was highly rated by those Kenyans familiar with it. So when the novelty of our new surroundings had lost its initial impact, and all companies had moved into their respective areas of responsibility, one resident correspondent of St George's Gazette was able to report:

> Patrolling is going on well. Rhino, buffalo, cheetah, zebra, giraffe, leopard, baboons, ostrich, monkey and pig have all been seen, but so far no Mau Mau have been encountered in this area.

Another contributor, from Support Company, after coming to grips with his new role, wrote that Mau Mau chasing did not require anti-tank guns or carriers, but feet, eyes and a rifle. In the meantime there had been noted 'with great appreciation, the kindness and hospitality of the local inhabitants who are ever willing to extend to us the warmth of their homes and the invaluable use of their bathrooms'.

It was perhaps inevitable for operational reasons that our introduction to Kenya's forest took the course it did so soon after our arrival, committed as we were to the restoration of law and order over a wide area. It was one of those situations where the mere presence of troops suppressed trouble, and the malcontents tended to melt away, if only to become a nuisance elsewhere.

Against this background there emerged some unexpected advantages, one of which arose from the opportunities that fusiliers had, whether they were on patrol, manning observation posts or off duty, to use their initiative. For while the Mau Mau moved in the forest mainly at night, their couriers, and those who were distributing ammunition or rations, sometimes did so by day, relying on their ability to avoid being spotted and using their own highly developed senses to detect those lying in wait for them. Indeed, such were their initial advantages in the early stages of our confrontation that we had to face the need to develop our own inherent instincts to match those who lived closer to nature. In this we had the invaluable assistance of the King's African Rifles, who had no difficulty in improving our level of jungle prowess; for it was remarkable how easily our Northumbrian countrymen adapted themselves to the Kenyan forest and set the necessary example to those of their comrades who had been brought up in more populated areas.

The requirement for tracking skills led to the attachment of eight native hunters, all of whom were proficient trackers, with sufficient ability to pass on the elements of their expertise to others. Fieldcraft was given a major boost through the formation of tracker combat teams, at least one of which existed within each unit. These consisted of six picked men, augmented by two African trackers plus a tracker-dog and handler. Each team was commanded by an officer specially trained in the skills involved, together with the use of the resources at his disposal and knowledge of Mau Mau fieldcraft. The ultimate refinement in withholding every possible source of assistance to the opposition meant reducing the natural gap between us whenever and however possible. Among the perfectionists this even included the discouragement of using any soap, lotion or disinfectant.

However, in the early stages it was striking how few of our men grasped the vital importance of two basic requirements for all who manned our OPs: the first was absolute silence and the second was complete stillness. These elementary needs may sound straightforward, but they have to be considered in the light of the exceptional faculties developed by African forest-dwellers. Such was the need for stillness, which is the main ingredient of silence under these conditions, that it became a matter of personal discipline, in the knowledge that the slightest movement could betray the existence of a planned ambush. Until this simple though vital fact had been absorbed by all involved it remained a problem, and there was no way of demonstrating the truth of this edict because it depended upon mental concentration. But once the required standard had been achieved, there were obvious advantages for the soldiers in their leisure time as well as when they were on duty. Also of assistance in this respect was a helpful pocket-size publication of some 160 pages entitled 'A Handbook of Anti-Mau Mau Operations', in which the section headed 'Big Game' had a practical ring throughout and commanded attention from its opening statement:

1. There is no doubt that big game in the Kenya forests are a more apparent danger than the Mau Mau to inexperienced troops. If the following simple facts are borne in mind, however, the apprehension of newcomers to the forest will be relieved:-

a) Elephant and buffalo have excellent senses of hearing and smell, and will usually move away if human beings are about.
b) All big game usually keep to game tracks and, therefore, provided camp is made off the game track and in thick bush, there is relatively little danger.

2. Elephant, buffalo and rhino are, however, particularly dangerous in areas which have been recently bombed. In these circumstances they frequently charge on sight and particular precautions are necessary.

I also had the benefit of Abel Chapman's guidance, which appears in his final book entitled *Retrospect*, published in 1928, under the heading 'Scent – Elephants'. Here he stresses the importance of wind direction and cites the occasion when he and his brother were approached from an upwind direction to within fourteen yards by a herd of unsuspecting elephants which, had the wind direction been reversed, would have detected their presence from probably a mile away. All this, and much more guidance, came our way as we prepared for an operational role determined by events which were giving the impression of what is known to seasoned troops as 'proper soldiering'. This, to the uninitiated, may be misleading, because it was intended to convey an acceptable blend of warlike and sporting activities. Kenya, indeed, provided just that for all those who were not actively engaged, or who were on only the periphery of current operations. When possible, sporting prospects tended to dominate our outlook, and much thought had been given by enthusiasts during the planning and preparations leading up to our departure from the United Kingdom. Valuable advice also came our way from one or two members of those regiments which had previously completed a tour of duty in the colony.

In the event, I believe there was no doubt that in our duties we covered everything that was expected of us; but when, thereafter, sporting prospects came into the reckoning, what a choice they presented! Here was a field of interest that appealed to many of us, and such was its scope that, while customary games and sports carried on wherever the demand existed, those with a wider outlook found the most varied field sports we could have wished for, particularly as our battalion's area of responsibility covered approximately 1,400 square miles, in which sporting opportunities commenced within walking distance of our camps. This not only appealed to enthusiasts, but incidentally enabled the cook to mention at lunchtime, "I could do with another guineafowl to make them go round at dinner, sir." Such requests could usually be promptly met.

When it came to sporting priorities, there was a clear code of practice, which included an embargo on the shooting of 'big game' either for sport or trophies; but any game 'for consumption' was acceptable, together with all the sport attached to it. This category included buck, which were numerous, so venison featured on many menus, as did guineafowl, francolin and duck. Throughout our time in Kenya those of us who were keen on shooting probably spent more time in pursuit of guineafowl than any other species. Nor was there any problem in finding beaters, most of whom, in my case, were Fusiliers who regarded beating as recreation, with a guineafowl each as a bonus at the end of the day. This would be roasted over a camp fire before being consumed and, only if necessary, shared with a mate. Considering that each bird's average weight before preparation was over three pounds, either way the men had a good supper, having possibly missed lunch while beating.

Had there, at the time or later, been a vote within our small group of enthusiasts to determine the most popular species I believe the guineafowl might have won, although on a 'cartridges fired' basis the East African francolin, a type of partridge, also had a strong following. However, as there were reputed to be more than a hundred species and sub-species of this bird, what we needed, and lacked, was a specialist to help with identification and to save us being left in doubt concerning exactly what we had accounted for during a successful day. Eventually I acquired all the necessary written guidance and photographs, and thereafter had no further problems of recognition that I can recall. Such research did, however, contribute to the interest we shared, including the satisfaction we experienced through the practice of using back guns when walking up guineafowl, which unlike most game birds often sat tight under cover, thereby permitting guns to walk past them, before they rose in order to make their escape rearwards. Another characteristic they had, often to their disadvantage, was to announce their intention by cackling just before rising, so alerting guns in their vicinity.

In retrospect, therefore, guineafowl earned a place of honour in many game registers, although one occasion did not reflect entirely favourably on those involved. This was when my party of soldier beaters persuaded me to extend a search for several guineafowl shot shortly before dusk and not yet picked. "Just a minute, sir, and we'll have the lot", came the entreaty. However, at that latitude in Kenya, so near the Equator, dusk is very brief and darkness falls within a few minutes. On the day in question I had, unusually, not brought a compass with me, and our dalliance left us waiting in the forest for the moon to rise two hours later, before we could see well enough to make our way back to camp. There are, of course, better ways of coming to terms with tropical forests and jungles, and their rules need to be heeded.

Another significant sporting attraction that came our way in Kenya was duck shooting, the best of which would take up to an hour to reach in a Jeep along rutted roads and tracks. There, as in numerous other distant locations, we had a choice of flooded and marshy areas to choose from. Usually the longer they took to reach the better the sport we had, which was just what most experienced wildfowlers in that region would expect. One of these areas, named Ol Belossat, had a landscaped dam where one of my better evening flights yielded five yellow-billed duck, five pochard and two teal. Ten days later, at Isiolo in the Northern Frontier Province, in addition to guineafowl I also shot a number of francolin. There was, indeed, no end to the fascination and enjoyment known to those who revelled in such a choice of sport.

As well as game shooting there was also trout fishing, which was equally memorable, being as good as any I can remember anywhere. During the Emergency, access to the forest was closed to all except members of the security forces in order to prevent accidents caused through settlers being mistaken for Mau Mau, who invariably presented fleeting targets and were therefore engaged without challenge. One consequence of this arrangement was that in such areas the settlers, for their own safety, were prevented from fishing for trout in all water courses within the forest. In fact, most of them had more than enough problems arising from the Emergency to dispel any sporting interests, and such were the priorities and restrictions that they may not even have had the inclination. By contrast, members of the security forces who were off duty, and happened to have a fishing rod with them, were free to make use of it for either rainbow or brown trout. Even so, discretion was essential, and those of us who took advantage of these opportunities needed to have our wits about us, for one cannot defend oneself if caught with no more than a fishing rod. This caution was not only necessary with regard to the possible unseen presence of Mau Mau; there was an occasion when one of our enthusiasts became aware that he was fishing under the close scrutiny of a leopard on the opposite bank of a narrow forest stream. It was natural in the circumstances that we subsequently took advantage of offers from armed volunteers to accompany us. One of my companions was a Fusilier whose home was in Felton, on the Northumbrian River Coquet, with which we were both familiar as salmon and sea trout addicts. Such a close sporting relationship contributed enormously to my enjoyment of the fishing, and the company of an armed escort meant that my conscience was not noticeably afflicted by any feeling of irresponsibility. Moreover, the memory of some of the most pleasurable and successful trout fishing of my life lingers still.

Chapter 17

The Magic of Grouse

One's first grouse, one's first salmon, or stag or wild goose, or other notable achievement, must ever remain a cherished memory.

Abel Chapman

It was early in my life that I realised how much grouse shooting meant to my father. From our family home close to the county boundary between Durham and Northumberland there were grouse moors to the north, south and west. Several of my father's close friends shared his interest, and this led to what later became recognised as a small syndicate, although, unlike many modern equivalents, the organisation and paperwork were limited to the exchange of a list of shooting dates and a cheque in return. Behind the scenes, one or two members would have agreed terms with the landowners and farmers involved and discussed dates, beaters and other essentials with the gamekeeper; this was between the two World Wars when the tempo of country life was still free from modern complexities. As a young child I only remember two cars in our neighbourhood; one belonged to the doctor and the other to my father. Consistent with this relaxed regime, country pursuits followed a course more in keeping with the Victorian era than current times.

Fortunately for my father, who was a busy man, he was generally able to arrange his commitments in such a way as to enjoy much of the sport in prospect, and many days might be spent in honour of St Grouse, beginning on the Twelfth of August and continuing thereafter on Saturdays until late autumn. I was thrilled at the prospect of accompanying him as soon as I was old enough, and so my sporting horizons widened appreciably. By then I had often watched the meticulous preparations that preceded his every shooting day, and before long I was enjoying my introduction to driven grouse as a young spectator; in this way, I soon realised the importance of safety as I noticed how my father and his neighbouring guns refrained from shooting at approaching low birds when in line with other guns within range. It was also explained to me how vulnerable guns in butts can be to the shooting of those on either side of them, should there be any lapses in judgement or procedure. It was pointed out to me that the same care is necessary when beaters are approaching and about to come within range. Many years later the practice was introduced of fixing vertical sticks to the sides of butts to assist guns in keeping their arc of fire within safe limits. I assume that the growing popularity of grouse shooting over the years, and, possibly, less safety training for guns, may have contributed to more accidents than the very rare instances of former times. It would be interesting, though probably impossible to achieve, to see an analysis of shotgun accidents according to the age and experience of the participants.

I was only once a witness to a dangerous shot, which resulted in the occupant of a neighbouring butt receiving a pellet in his cheek. Following a discussion on the spot the offending guest was asked to leave, and the incident cast a gloom over the remaining middle-aged and elderly guns, among whom it became the sole topic of conversation for the rest of the day, even continuing over the telephone as soon as they had returned home. At the time I was on leave from my regiment following nine years of active service and regarded a stray shotgun pellet in rather a different light. Without disagreeing that safety must be of paramount importance, I perhaps took a less grave view of this unfortunate mishap.

As a boy, before the Second World War, I would be a spectator for some five weeks of a grouse season, which coincided with my school holidays. These weeks included the opening and most prolific part of the season, during which I accompanied my father and made myself as useful as I could in marking fallen birds, in partnership with an experienced and dedicated spaniel, which at that stage had probably retrieved more grouse than I had ever seen. It was an invaluable introduction, and I used to return to school for the Michaelmas term with a glow of enthusiasm sufficient to maintain my interest until the following season.

When I was considered old and responsible enough to carry a gun on these occasions, my father sought the approval of his friends before permitting me to accompany him; at this stage he ensured that I was always placed on a flank of the line of guns, with himself in the adjoining butt. It was on one of these early occasions that my first red-letter day on a grouse moor occurred. The line of butts stretched up the side of a large moorland feature, from a watercourse at the bottom up to the skyline on my left. As the lowest gun, I had a distant view along the valley stretching away in front of me. In due course the beaters' white flags came into view, at which stage my attention was concentrated on the intervening landscape of purple heather from which grouse were anticipated. When the beaters were still about half a mile from me I spotted two black dots in the sky, high enough to catch my eye. They appeared to be flying towards me, and before long I recognised them as blackcock, the name used by most guns for the larger black grouse, as distinct from the more numerous red grouse. As the gap narrowed they began to climb as though they had seen the line of guns, but they maintained their course, following the stream beside which my butt was situated and offering me the chance of a right and left, which, for the benefit of the uninitiated, is shooting parlance for success with both barrels. To my gratification the two birds fell dead behind me, and in the windless conditions an unaccustomed ripple of applause reached me from the butts above. Naturally, perhaps, the memory of that brace of 'black' has never faded.

I have always regarded blackgame with interest, partly because they are rarely present in significant numbers. However, in the *Moor and Marsh* volume on shooting by Lord Walsingham and Sir Ralph Payne-Gallwey, published in 1886, in the Badminton Library series, the perspective was quite different: 'Only a few years ago Black game were found in almost every county in England, even in Middlesex.' It is recorded in 1860 that 252 were shot in one day in Cannock Chase, Staffordshire. In the intervening decades there has been a steady decline, but on some shooting estates steps are being taken to reverse this situation by releasing blackcock under a Game Conservancy Trust national project. As a result of this it was reported in 2007 that, among other areas, there was a good spread of black grouse from Alston to Hexham.

The occasion when I shot my brace of blackcock was before the Second World War, and it was not until more than ten years later that I was able to resume driven grouse shooting, following a long period of overseas service. Then, almost as a gesture from the Fates after a further seven years abroad, in 1957 I found myself in command of my regimental depot on the outskirts of Newcastle-upon-Tyne and only ten miles from where I was born and grew up. There I was favourably placed within reach of grouse moors, the owners of which were known either to me or to others in the regiment. Either way, I was highly fortunate, and there followed some of the best grouse shooting I ever enjoyed, mostly among friends whom I knew well.

Today, more than half a century later, many such grouse moors still come readily to my mind, and my shooting diary aids the process. Of those in my shooting records none stands higher than Whitfield Moor in Northumberland, which covers an extensive area between Hexham and Alston. There, during the third quarter of the last century, I was frequently privileged to join the Blackett-Ord family, and to me it remains unique, because the components of a successful and enjoyable grouse shoot are many and complex and Whitfield, in my view, had them all. One day in particular stands out in my memory, and no doubt it came at the apex of a disease-free period, for grouse populations have their troughs as well as their peaks. At one stage, as the guns were approaching the line of butts for the next drive, Jock Blackett-Ord, the brother-in-law of my great friend Charles Mitchell, commented: "You should enjoy yourself here, Dare; on the last occasion the gun did very well." My butt, known as the Pulpit, was noticeably elevated above those on either side, and from it I had an all-round view, so during the occasional pauses in the shooting, which was intense, I was able to glance along the line to observe what was happening on either side of me. However, the tempo of activity was maintained until the beaters came within range, and only then could the guns relax.

When this drive came to an end I realised it had been an exceptional experience, although the full extent was not clear until later. In the meantime, efforts were directed towards the task of picking up, in which all dogs were deployed. After some fifteen minutes the guns, together with their dogs, had to move off to the next drive, leaving a picker-up with his dogs to complete the task. It transpired later that my share of the bag at that drive was estimated at no fewer than sixty grouse, and the Pulpit remains prominent among my shooting memories.

A remarkable incident occurred during a day when I was shooting grouse as my father's guest on one of the moors where he regularly shot. In the course of one drive I wounded a grouse enough to affect its flight, causing it to swerve to the right as it lost height. However, at this point I had to stop watching it before it reached the ground, so did not see where it fell. Later in the same drive I was surprised by a wounded grouse that appeared from my left and flew into my butt through the rear entrance, having been shot by my neighbour, and then completed a turn before expiring at my feet. When the drive ended I took this grouse with the intention of handing it to the neighbouring gun who had shot it; but on my way to his butt I noticed him walking towards me and presumed he was coming to collect it. As he came nearer I saw he was also carrying a grouse, and when we met he explained that he realised I had shot it because it had flown into his butt from the rear after he had heard me firing. I then told him my identical story, and as we exchanged grouse we agreed we had experienced an extraordinary, and possibly unique, coincidence.

So far this account has referred to the conventional method of driving grouse with a team of beaters under the direction of an experienced keeper who has the necessary qualities and knowledge to present grouse over the guns. However, comparable experience is also called for when it comes to the less formal sport of shooting grouse in rough and hilly moorland terrain, where the use of a full team of beaters would be neither necessary nor practicable. Under such conditions success lies with smaller parties of guns surmounting the difficulties, sometimes walking with intervening beaters, and here local knowledge is essential, preferably with the instinct of how grouse are likely to behave in such conditions when flushed.

This requirement I had met at an earlier stage with my father when walking up grouse on the North Yorkshire moors, where uneven ground necessitated instant reaction and retention of balance when grouse took flight. Thereafter it was not until 1943, when I was stationed in Dumfriesshire, that I was able to undertake this pastime again, and then I experienced the need to adjust to wartime variations. I had been posted as chief instructor of the 3rd Division Battle School, which was about to arrive from a less suitable location in the South of England. I was required to set up the various wings of the school within a wide area around the small town of Moffat, in addition to which there was a street-fighting wing some fifty miles to the north-west in a requisitioned part of Glasgow, using live ammunition, grenades and explosives while, simultaneously, normal life carried on in the adjoining streets.

In the meantime I had been authorised to assess a considerable area of Dumfriesshire, north of Moffat, in which field firing by artillery and live firing from tanks could take place as part of the Army's pre-invasion training prior to D-Day. This called for a period of extensive reconnaissance in order to familiarise myself with the mountainous terrain, and the only way to do it was through personal exploration. In this instance I was provided with a fell pony, of which I made much use. However, parts of the country were too precipitous even for my mount, and these had to be traversed on foot, enabling me to take my 12 bore and Dinah, who had been reunited with me from her temporary home with my parents in Northumberland. As I became more familiar with the terrain I met more grouse. At first it was during the close season, and I never met grouse that were tamer. At times it was as if they were more interested in me than vice versa. However, following 12 August this relationship changed, notwithstanding the fact that the grouse were unaware that in my capacity as temporary custodian of this vast area I was the only person, as far as I knew, authorised under wartime restrictions to carry a shotgun. I had to keep my sporting interests in proportion to the need to train thousands of troops for the invasion of Europe; but in the circumstances my conscience remained clear, as Dinah and I confined our pursuit of grouse to those occasions when military duties required my presence in the hills and the terrain precluded the use of all vehicles. We had some memorable sport in the course of essential tactical reconnaissance, occasionally quite spontaneously. One day, when planning a new phase of battle training on moorland that we had not previously utilised, I went out accompanied by a small group of NCO instructors. We were all dressed and armed as we would be in battle and, as we were familiarising ourselves with the lie of the land, two or three grouse rose in front of us, just as they might have done during a grouse drive. On the spur of the moment, and without serious intent, I drew my revolver from its holster and fired at the nearest grouse, which by then was not less than 20 yards away. Against incalculable odds it fell stone dead. Thereafter, my task was to conceal my own surprise and play it down as an example of the standard of marksmanship we were seeking from those under our instruction.

Sightings of grouse were also a part of my life that I was permitted to share with my parents. In a letter home dated 26 March 1943 I wrote:

Today, with another instructor, I climbed the highest mountain for many miles round here – 'White Coomb', 2,696 feet. It made a lovely climb and towards the top was very steep, so much so that we had to tread delicately, like Agag, and rest frequently. After reaching the top we climbed down about 1,000 feet to a lovely little loch, Loch Skeen, hidden right up in these hills and itself a long climb from the nearest road, two miles away. All round the loch, which is about half a mile long and 300–400 yards wide, were grouse and yet more grouse. They were everywhere and in every case except one they were paired. One literally could not walk more than 100 yards without putting up a pair. They were very tame and you could see them standing up on crests all around. Several flew over the loch in the sunlight – a lovely sight; they flew all round us and sometimes directly over us as if taunting us out of season.

In a matching context, George Malcolm and Aymer Maxwell, in their book *Grouse and Grouse Moors*, published in 1910, wrote: 'This pleasant border land is no fit stage for the set pieces of shooting; loaders, luncheon tents, and ladies would be as out of place here as a life guardsman's trappings on a predatory Cossack, but it is the country of all others wherein to wage the guerrilla warfare of sport.'

Soon after the war it was sandgrouse in the Middle East rather than British red and black grouse that came my way, but when the Palestine Mandate ended in 1948 a welcome spell of home service followed, before my next overseas posting, allowing me many splendid days shooting grouse. As time passed, my good fortune continued when I was able to arrange a period of leave to coincide with the early part of another season. However, such opportunities gradually diminished; my parents moved south and I eventually retired from the Army. Home was established in the south-west, and although grouse had been introduced to Exmoor they never flourished and after years of decline they died out. There comes a time for all ageing sportsmen when they have to accept that adjustment to change, whether in advancing years or availability of sport, is inevitable. And so, in my own case, wildfowling and grouse shooting were slowly phased out, leaving the records and a host of memories to enjoy.

Chapter 18

The Charm of Ptarmigan

'The charms of a day after ptarmigan lie not so much in the actual shooting, as in the strange and unfamiliar surroundings in which the scene is laid.' I cannot imagine any experienced ptarmigan enthusiast who would not accept the sentiment behind this view expressed by George Malcolm and Aymer Maxwell.

Although the ptarmigan, which is referred to in the *Handbook of British Birds* as the Scottish ptarmigan, is only distantly related to the slightly larger red grouse, nevertheless they have much in common, and it is not unusual to find them sharing the same moorland habitat. In such cases, however, the ptarmigan are almost invariably established on higher ground, with the grouse below them. This explains, at least in part, why ptarmigan feature more consistently in the bags of remote and elevated grouse moors and why nearly all of them are accounted for by guns walking rather than shooting driven birds from butts. I had not gained much experience in the pursuit of this species before I realised how much interest surrounds the bird, its habitat and the magnificent settings in which it is usually found, all too often with enemies in the offing. Principal among the latter are golden eagles, which are acceptable to most of us, and foxes, which are not. Sportsmen on the whole are less of a threat, because the high, rocky ground preferred by the ptarmigan is unknown to most guns who frequent grouse moors. It follows, by and large, that the most successful ptarmigan shots are among the fittest and most committed enthusiasts.

My own introduction to ptarmigan was in Perthshire, where for some years after the Second World War I was invited by Charles Mitchell to join him for holidays at Ardeonaig, a sporting estate he had acquired on the south side of Loch Tay. The moor ascended to over 2,000 feet, and conveniently nearby on the lochside road was the small and isolated Ardeonaig Hotel. This had all the desirable facilities for a small shooting party not exceeding five guns, and neither comfort nor cuisine could be faulted, particularly since Charles had brought all the wine required for the week from the extensive cellars at Pallinsburn, his home in Northumberland. However, from the outset it was clear to us that the highest standard of fitness was essential, for the mountainous terrain was more than a little demanding in terms of physical effort. As often as not we would limit our shooting to half a day, as on 11 September 1957, when in three and a half hours our party of five guns accounted with satisfaction for twenty-three grouse, one blackcock and two hares, illustrating how little connection there need be between the enjoyment of a day's shooting and the size of the bag.

From time to time we would climb high enough to meet ptarmigan, and the more I saw of them the more fascinating I found them, almost, though not quite, to the point of losing my wish to shoot them. There is, apparently, no accurate way of determining the extent to which the sporting fraternity deplete the stock of ptarmigan, and it remains a matter of judgement based on experience. My own records lack continuity but leave me with a clear conscience as one gun within an average group of four. While our bag of grouse was usually respectable, we never reached double figures for ptarmigan on any day during our annual week in residence.

I learned, not without some surprise, how tame ptarmigan can appear when confronted, possibly for the first time, by a human being who, it seems, they do not view instinctively as an enemy. That certainly was the conclusion I reached when it appeared that I could have surprised a full covey of ptarmigan sheltering among rocks within a few yards of me. In reality it is far more likely that they are aware of those closing in on them; but it is in their nature to sit tighter than most other game birds and, as part of this practice, they have a remarkable aptitude for making use of ground that blends with their plumage. They exploit this ability particularly during the breeding season, when they are reluctant to leave nests containing either eggs or chicks. Thus they rely on their natural plumage, which not only blends into the background of heather during most of the year, but later turns to white as the winter snows approach.

The limited awareness shown by some visiting sportsmen is likely to be in contrast with the sensitivity of the shepherds and gamekeepers who have grown up in proximity to the natural world, many of whom have developed an instinct that enables them to locate ptarmigan nests which, as scrapes in the ground, would be invisible to the less observant. Hen birds are apt to remain motionless on their nests and may stay for as long as necessary in the presence of visitors. Some will be sheltering young, and the curiosity of observers should be restrained and nature allowed to follow its course. Indeed, the continuing wellbeing of the ptarmigan is largely assured by its relative inaccessibility to homo sapiens.

A further element in the protection of ptarmigan is the fact that they are largely limited to the mountainous ground of Perthshire and the other Highland counties, which is more familiar to deer stalkers than to grouse shooters; and where the land is reserved for stalking the use of shotguns is often discouraged. Ardeonig was perhaps unusual in that we were able to participate in both grouse shooting and deer stalking, as well as salmon fishing on Loch Tay. One morning when we were setting out after grouse, Charles asked me to take the left flank on which there was a ridge of higher ground. Perhaps in the anticipation of surprising ptarmigan I climbed with caution, which was just as well because less than a hundred yards beyond the ridge was a handsome stag, apparently unaware of my presence. I withdrew with additional care, and Charles, having noted this through his binoculars, joined me to see what had prompted my withdrawal. Fortunately, his deer rifle was to hand and he offered it to me. To be presented with a strange weapon, together with a couple of rounds of ammunition, at such a moment is not the ideal introduction to a successful stalk; but all worked out according to plan, and today the stag's antlers, mounted at home, serve as a reminder of those happy days, and of Charles who died so prematurely as a result of wounds received in Korea.

My fascination with the ptarmigan has been reflected in the writings of countless naturalists. In his *History of British Birds*, dated 1853, the Reverend F. O. Morris extols the ptarmigan with lyrical enthusiasm:

True Children of the mist, and free as the pure air they breathe, the Ptarmigans frequent the upper parts and summits of the highest mountains, where utter desolation reigns around, and nature is seen in the most wild and savage beauty. These scenes they never leave – the mountaineer's love for his native mountain is stronger than any other 'Love of one's country'. In extremely severe and stormy weather they come a little lower down, or take advantage of the shelter of the clefts that are met with in some lonely glen, but never cease to be birds of the snow.

Today it is no longer widely known what a numerous species the ptarmigan was in former times, though many records have survived that classify it as one of Britain's most prolific gamebirds, and thousands were once consigned to London during the ptarmigan's extended season. Morris reveals that during 1839 one dealer alone shipped six thousand to London and two thousand to Liverpool, while a salesman in Leadenhall Market received fifteen thousand. Further afield, a prominent sportsman stated that 'a dealer in Norway will dispose of fifty thousand in a season', while another participant calculated that sixty thousand had been killed during one winter in Lapland.

With this evidence one can only assume that, in the course of the intervening decades since 1839, changes in land use, coupled with improved access and increased disturbance in those parts of Britain formerly associated with this captivating bird, have all combined against the ptarmigan's interests. Nevertheless, and notwithstanding these pressures, the ptarmigan has retained its special status in the eyes of those sportsmen who care more for the nature of their endeavours than the size of the bags they take home.

After my experiences at Ardeonaig, the next time I met ptarmigan they were cousins of those I had found so beguiling in Scotland. Twenty years had passed, and I was exploring Lapland in Northern Norway with my wife. I found the spell they cast had in no way diminished; rather was it stronger, when coupled with the attractions of elk within the Arctic Circle. The only minor problem we met was our ineligibility, as visitors, to extend our range of observation through the use of snow-scooters, riding which was limited to local inhabitants, who used them for transport as well as hunting and fishing.

Chapter 19

Woodcock, Snipe and the Minstrel of the Moors

A lthough it might be difficult to substantiate, I have the impression that, with the possible exception of grouse, there are more stories concerning woodcock than any other game bird. Assuming this to be the case, might one not hope to find a consensus of views as to why this is so? In the meantime, most experienced shots will stand by their own convictions.

Edward Grey (1862-1933), who later became Viscount Grey of Fallodon, was one of the most distinguished statesmen of his day and was also a keen bird-lover. In his book *The Charm of Birds* he recalls how one fine day by the Northumbrian sea shore towards the end of November he saw a woodcock arrive, evidently from a great height, with considerable velocity behind its descent ('It slanted down over me at tremendous speed ...'). The account continues with his impression of how these birds cross the North Sea quite easily and without showing any signs of fatigue on arrival. His is but one theory about this fascinating game bird, on which agreement, even among knowledgeable observers, is patchy. For example, the Lonsdale Library volume on *Shooting by Moor, Field and Shore*, published in 1934, expresses the view that, 'Woodcock are usually in the last stages of exhaustion on arrival, and at Blakeney, on the east coast of Norfolk, they have been picked up in the main street.' This difference of opinion is just one example of how the most dedicated students of nature can on occasion be at variance in their conclusions, even when these are based on assiduous observation. However, it has been the opinion of a high proportion of the most experienced shots in

Britain over many years that the woodcock is unique among game birds for the respect and interest it commands.

The average weight of a woodcock is around 12 ounces, and in addition to its sporting attributes it is renowned for its culinary excellence. At the end of any day's shooting during which woodcock have been bagged, guns who have accounted for them may experience a glow of satisfaction. Those who maintain records of their sport may mention their contribution on such occasions, and among Northumbrians such additions to the bag may be more likely than in counties further west. This is because the majority of woodcock shot in Britain are migrants from Scandinavia, and because they are committed by nature to migrate seasonally, it is by instinct that they choose the shortest route across the North Sea; this accounts for the presence of more woodcock in the North East during the autumn than elsewhere in England. Some woodcock remain in Britain throughout the year, and it is usually in the summer that the males' display flight, known as 'roding', can be seen at dawn and dusk, before they head off to feed in some area of boggy or marshy land where they penetrate the ground with their long beaks in search of worms.

I recollect that when I was a boy my father and his friends always showed interest in the number of woodcock in the bag, and particularly if this occurred early in the season. Very occasionally the opportunity would arise for a gun to achieve a 'right and left' at woodcock, although I have never witnessed it. The closest I came to it personally was when I shot a woodcock with my first barrel and, as I was reloading, heard the shout 'Mark cock' from a neighbouring gun. This I also managed to shoot, but it did not count as a right and left. I belong to one of successive generations who were shown by their fathers or elders how to find and remove the 'pin feather' from the leading edge of each wing of a woodcock. This became a habit during that era when more family shoots existed than is the case today, and in modern times some guns are unaware of the custom. It would be interesting to know how the tradition developed of collecting these pin feathers. It may have been because for centuries they have been in demand by fly-tiers and artists specialising in fine painting, particularly of miniature portraits. I am one of the many guns who collected them in the days when, except on the smartest of shoots, guns tended to gather up at the end of each drive what they had individually shot; this practice still continues on many smaller shoots. Such a system provides a pause in proceedings that allows an opportunity to extract the pin feathers from woodcock, most of which, in my case, used to be transferred into the band around my deerstalker. When the hat, which had served me longer than I can remember, reached the end of its long life, the pin feathers were extracted before it was disposed of. Some feathers had failed to withstand the rigours of the intervening years, and the gaps they left were still apparent, but the survivors, the oldest of which had seen more than 70 seasons, today live on within an appendage to my current game diary, where they catch the eye and steal my thoughts.

As one might expect from even one individual's study of a single species, based on a cross section of helpful reports, some interesting impressions will emerge, for the woodcock is indeed a fascinating bird. My own earliest source of information, now almost two hundred years after its publication in 1819, is *The Shooter's Guide* by B. Thomas, which remains a fine record and has retained its appeal as well as its relevance to the pioneering era of shooting for sport. The 300 pages of this volume are in more than one sense a classic account of the sport's early days and the manner in which it took shape. Among the hundreds, if not thousands, of shooting books, it must surpass most of its contemporaries through its author's comprehension of an ancient sport. Eight of its pages concern woodcock, which it reveals can be remarkably tame while incubating its eggs. As an example of this, Thomas mentions how one person, having found a woodcock sitting on its nest, would stand over it and stroke it. Notwithstanding this liberty, the parent hatched its young and in due course disappeared with them.

Twenty-three years after the publication of *The Shooter's Guide* came *The Modern Shooter* by Captain Lacy, published in 1842, which in my view is a shooting classic. Moreover, unlike the vast majority of early books on shooting, it contains some refreshing humour, an example of which relates to a gun's personal experience while shooting in the extensive grounds of his own home. He fired at a woodcock that was flying in the general direction of his house, some quarter of a mile distant. His account reveals that the bird, though evidently hit – and this was later confirmed – continued to maintain 'the even tenor of its way'. Shortly afterwards, when passing the house in further pursuit of it, he was informed that 'a very remarkable thing had just taken place': a woodcock, some minutes earlier, had fallen close to the kitchen door and had been bagged by the cook! It was presumed that, having failed to clear the house, it had struck the building, thereby falling virtually into the hands of the party who was most conveniently placed to make use of it.

Curious as it may be, one of my favourite memories of woodcock is of an occasion when I was without a gun. It was in the late 1930s, when I was at home on holiday from school. Initially it was a litter of young fox cubs that had attracted my interest as they emerged from their earth at dusk in order to play. I had walked from the house, down across a couple of fields to the edge of a favourite patch of woodland, to watch the cubs I had previously discovered. So fascinating were they from the outset that I cannot now remember at what stage the counter-attraction intervened, but I was suddenly aware of the presence of woodcock roding through the trees that concealed me from them. With amazing agility the birds swooped in a series of low circuits, following a wavering course before disappearing along a drive cut through the wood.

Another interesting and, I believe, possibly unique characteristic of woodcock that I would love to have seen, though never did, is its ability to carry its young in flight. This curious habit has been well documented, though the precise way it is achieved varies in different accounts. It seems that they can be hugged between the thighs of the parent bird, or supported partly by the feet and partly by the bill. Ralph Payne-Gallwey may have been among the earliest authors to remark on it when he wrote in *The Fowler in Ireland*, published in 1882, that he had twice seen a woodcock carrying a young bird, 'huddled up under the neck'. He also described how he had watched them 'teaching their broods to wheel and sport in the air – a very pretty sight'.

Some of the woodcock I have bagged during my shooting experience were birds unfortunate enough to fly across the line of guns in a driven pheasant shoot, while others were achieved when rough shooting, either by myself or with just one or two friends. Part of the enjoyment of rough shooting by oneself is the opportunity to spend time watching the wildlife, and there were several occasions when I was struck with admiration for the woodcock's remarkable protective colouring, its plumage beautifully blending with the surrounding foliage. I have seen a bird land in a small patch of undergrowth and have carefully stalked it with every confidence that I had marked its exact location. Even when I widened the search I had to come to the conclusion that I must have been deceived in its landing place and have lost it. But when I then put a dog into the very area I had been scanning, the woodcock rose with a clap of wings and I realised I had been looking at the bird all the time without being able to distinguish its body from the cover it matched so well.

The woodcock can present a testing target, because of its rapid and sometimes twisting flight, but it is when planning to go snipe shooting that the message to guns really is, 'tune up your reflexes'. How one achieves this is a matter of opinion, but the short answer is, 'by practice'. Those sportsmen who are unfamiliar with snipe tend to develop a complex concerning the problem they present. At which moment and how exactly should they fire? By hesitating as they endeavour to shoot at 'zag' when they should have fired at 'zig', they continue to be unsuccessful, and the complex is deepened as the misses outnumber the hits. What has been lacking is the instinctive reaction to shoot before the bird has had time to develop the necessary momentum to demonstrate its agility, and this can only come with experience.

Of the three kinds of snipe known to British sportsmen the great, or solitary, snipe is so rare that for sporting purposes it can be discounted. This leaves the common, or full, snipe and the jack snipe, although of these two it is the former that is best known, not only to sportsmen but also to gourmets. However, it was not in the British Isles but in Northern Palestine that I enjoyed the best possible snipe shooting, in the extensive, low lying, partially flooded area around Lake Hula. There, during weekends, small parties of guns from units belonging to the three British Army divisions stationed in Palestine at the time might turn their attention to snipe between the early morning and evening duck flights. During one weekend in December 1947 thirty guns, few of whom were experienced snipe shots, managed to account for over four hundred snipe within a total bag of nine hundred and ninety wildfowl, which contained no fewer than eight varieties of duck as well as white-fronted geese.

As frequently mentioned, one of our problems throughout that period was running out of cartridges, even following strict anti-pilferage measures, and my own expenditure of cartridges during those three years far exceeded that of any comparable period throughout my sporting life. Another problem was how to assist the few who were lacking experience when it came to the handling of a 12 bore shot gun but who wished to become better acquainted. There being no shooting school or professional supervision within reach, the tyros or duffers, of whom there were a few, were deprived of qualified guidance; so in these situations the shooting experience of others was called upon. It is at such times that the thought may pass through one's mind, 'at least I can't make him any worse'!

My final member of this illustrious trio of birds is the captivating curlew, known in Scotland as the whaup, and aptly referred to by some imaginative admirer as a 'minstrel', on account of its easily recognisable, liquid, bubbling call. A characteristic of snipe is the drumming sound they make in rapid flight when, for whatever reason, they dive, singly, into the wind. The curlew, however, calls at any time of day, but its song is most notable in the evening when, under still conditions, it can carry as far as two miles and can be ear-piercing if heard close by. What wildfowler of former times who, like me, has traversed the saltings for years, could remain oblivious to this evocative call when hearing it again.

The common curlew (as distinct from the stone curlew) is the largest of all the European waders and used to be a sporting bird until, in 1981, it was put on the protected list owing to its declining numbers, due to the expansion of farming in its moorland breeding grounds. As I write, it is seventy-three years since I shot my first curlew, but still I can recapture some of the tension that stalking them generated in my younger days. It is among the wariest of birds, and outwitting one was regarded by wildfowlers as a great challenge. Thinking back over my own experience, I was considerably reassured when I read the words of J. E. Harting in his *Hints on Shore Shooting*, published in 1871: 'If you can see a Curlew within shot before he sees you, and can stalk and kill him, you may flatter yourself you are not a bad hand at shore shooting. To kill an old Curlew, except by a lucky chance, requires an amount of patience, endurance and stratagem that few who have not tried it would credit.' During and immediately after the Second World War, when all farmed meat was rationed, I was among the many wildfowlers who learned what a crafty and elusive bird it was to bag. However, in addition to its sporting challenge, it was comparable as a table bird to many species of duck, providing it had been shot when returning from feeding inland rather than on estuarial invertebrates – and even then some cooks were more imaginative and successful than others!

Chapter 20

Rabbits and Rough Shooting

It was with my parents' encouragement that I developed the practice of observing wild creatures, and rabbits soon became part of this interest, which began quite early in life. During school holidays I spent many evenings in woodland belonging to my father, but only once did I meet strangers in it, when I surprised several poachers ferreting rabbits. Being presumably intent on avoiding recognition, they departed in haste, leaving me with a number of nets to recover. As I was doing this a ferret emerged from the warren and was so docile that I was able to catch it and put it securely in its box abandoned nearby. Thereafter, ferreting became quite an interest, as an addition to the traditional sport of rough shooting.

The arrival in Britain in 1953 of the disease myxomatosis was widely welcomed by most landowners and farmers, for whom rabbits had become a considerable pest. Before that, however, most rough shooting enthusiasts had relied on rabbits to enhance their sport, and some particular rabbits have remained in my memory. Although my earliest success had been achieved with a .410 shotgun in the woods at home, the first rabbit that really made an impression on me was at school, when I was nine years old. I have already described how my unorthodox headmaster permitted me to take out his .410 unsupervised within the school grounds, and how eventually one evening this permission was extended to the neighbouring farmland. I saw some rabbits in a field, but out of range, so I slowly stalked them under cover of a hedge and eventually achieved a clean kill. All the other rabbits of course immediately scampered for their burrows, so I returned to give the headmaster my report and hand in the gun, with one used and two unused cartridges. The memory of that particular rabbit has never dimmed, even though my total of rabbits shot over the years has reached well into four figures. There were two others a few years later that also made an impression, when my mother had brought me down to Exmoor for a short holiday after I had suffered at the hands of a particularly inept dentist. This was my first visit to the area that was eventually to become my home, and while my mother went hunting I accompanied a delightful retired farm worker who had permission to shoot rabbits on the local estate. One day I managed to shoot not one but two black rabbits and I was able to get the skins cured, so I had them made into a pair of gloves for my mother, whose birthday happened to be approaching. They were very special, and my wife has them now, still in excellent condition more than seventy-five years later. The only other black rabbit I ever saw was in September 1952 when my parents were living on the edge of Exmoor and I had returned home on leave. The last evening of my leave I noted in my game diary: 'Final night's take before lifting the traps was 6 rabbits, 1 rat, 1 grey squirrel. I shot 4 more rabbits on the Bracken Bank and saw 1 jet black half grown one.'

I eventually shot so many rabbits that unfortunately I got out of the way of recording them in my game register as part of a normal sporting routine. However, for a boy in the pre-war era, pitting one's wits against rabbits was very good training, and it became highly advantageous following the outbreak of war in 1939. In January 1940 meat rationing was introduced, and immediately the demand for rabbits spiralled as they became widely recognised as an acceptable substitute for more conventional, but scarce, cuts of meat. At its lowest point, meat rationing dropped to one shilling's worth (5p in modern currency) per person per week, so the distribution of game and rabbits, which were never put on the rationed list, became a significant aspect of shooting. As far as I can remember, no official guidelines existed for the disposal of surplus game, and one wonders what today's bureaucrats would have made of it. Back then, common sense prevailed, and it was left to those who had game in excess of their requirements to use their own judgement in its disposal. As a result, many elderly, sick and otherwise needy people benefited from such generosity, and although game is not to everyone's liking, rabbits were always welcome. In some places rooks were made use of in pies, but they had to be really young to be at all palatable.

During the war much of the control of rabbits and other vermin depended on youngsters and the more senior sportsmen, who were still fit and active enough to use a shotgun with effect. Organised shoots for syndicates were suspended because many of the pre-war participants were serving with HM Forces, and therefore rough shooting assumed a greater significance, with the demand for rabbits peaking to supplement the meat ration. Viewed retrospectively, it seems remarkable that as much sport was enjoyed as was the case, bearing in mind that many of those still at home in reserved occupations were working to capacity with limited assistance. Petrol rationing severely restricted the use of transport, and even when service personnel were home on leave they faced the problem of obtaining cartridges. The manufacture of shotgun ammunition virtually ceased during the war, and those who still had an opportunity to shoot, after using up what stocks still existed within the trade, had to borrow from generous friends who might have more than they needed. Against this background my father, whose business occupied much of his time, played his part, with the assistance of a retired gamekeeper, in keeping vermin from getting 'way out of hand'; but otherwise he only shot when necessary to produce something for the larder, unless either my brother Peter, who was serving in the Royal Navy, or I were on leave. However, his custody of the woods and fields around our home did much to ensure the availability of sport on the occasions when we were at home during the shooting season.

Apart from my visits home, however, I was fortunate, as mentioned earlier, in being twice stationed in Dumfriesshire. During the autumn, winter and spring of 1941-2 I was an instructor at a junior officers tactical school at Annan, and throughout 1943 I was the chief instructor of the 3rd Division battle school in Moffat. Within the live-firing training area in the remote, mountainous terrain many thousands of acres were closed to the general public and even to local authorities. My second appointment turned out to be one of the most professionally rewarding ones of my service career, with the addition of sport of a high order to enjoy when time permitted. Moreover, being a Battle School, the instructors as well as the students spent most of their time on duty dressed, armed and equipped as for war. This, in my case set the scene for an incident about which I wrote home to my parents on 22 March:

I have had a lot of exercise lately. Tomorrow morning I am taking the instructors for about ten miles cross country over the mountains. We are toughening up before the courses start. I am pretty fit already and am doing about 10 miles a day on average ... The moors are lifting with hares and rabbits; today I hit a rabbit at about 20 yards with my revolver and it was running too, which made it better still!

In the autumn, on 31 October, I had occasion to write home again about rough shooting:

Yesterday Guy Thornycroft and I had another capital day's shooting. We called it a 'bits and pieces' day and visited all the little bits of ground locally where we had permission to shoot. We hoped for about 20 head at the most and we were most surprised and not to say delighted when we got 47 head made up of pheasants (11), grouse, duck (Mallard and Teal), rabbits, hares and snipe. I can never remember a longer day or a harder day's shooting in my life; we both shot very well and I think between us we missed about 2 pheasants all day.

One of my duties at that Battle School was to make periodic visits to similar establishments widely scattered throughout the country in order to exchange ideas on course syllabuses and techniques, because guidance was still not forthcoming from a higher level. This arrangement worked in either direction and could follow a request or suggestion from any of those concerned. Sometimes it involved a long journey by jeep with an overnight stop, and it was surprising how many gun and tackle shops I was able to include in my itineraries. This was during the era in which gunsmiths were still numerous, so few towns were without at least one. I soon discovered that there was in many cases an imbalance between their supply of guns and cartridges, which is how I had been able, within only one year, to acquire 4, 8, 10 and 12 bore guns, usually without ammunition and therefore going cheap. The sequel was to find, cluttering a gunsmith's premises, job lots of ammunition for which he had no guns. Either way the prices were depressed by the lack of demand, while my problem was to persuade my parents to find somewhere to store them all at home.

The five years immediately following the war saw me in postings overseas, with only occasional spells of home leave, but in the autumn of 1950 the assignment that had taken me to the USA and Canada was approaching completion. By then my parents had moved south to Exmoor, and on 5 October I wrote them a lengthy letter, at the end of which came a slightly involved assortment of requests:

Now, before I close I wonder if you could do 3 things for me with as little delay as possible:

1. Hang all my snares out of doors to weather, i.e. to lose their smell and the new ones to lose their shine. I think they should be on the back of the workshop door – at least 60, if not 100.
2. Buy 3 dozen rabbit traps and bury them in damp soil to rust up and lose their smell. Let them stay until I raise them. A month underground is not too much. (N.B. No need to bother about either of these if you have already had a trapper on the place recently, or if the rabbits are no longer numerous.)
3. If the moor field bank next the road is still infested with rabbits, if possible take all the cattle and horses out so that the rabbit runs will be clearly defined in the grass.

And then, more light-heartedly:

4. Warn Peggy [Lakeland Terrier] she'll have a hard time of it tied up while the traps are set.
5. Warn Duchess [Labrador] that there's work ahead.
6. Warn the rabbits there's a hard time coming!

This challenge thrown down to the rabbits stayed in place until 1953, when myxomatosis arrived, after which the rabbit population plummeted; by 1955 it was estimated to have dropped by 95%. Before that time, however, safeguarding enough grass to feed their stock was an ongoing problem for farmers. As an example of how it appeared on the ground, on 2 September 1952 when I was once more home on leave I noted in my game diary: 'In the Great Meadow rabbits are now numbered by the hundred rather than the score. Just like a moving carpet.' A couple of weeks later I wrote: 'Left the house just before 7 o'clock to shoot a rabbit required for the table. Returned

11 minutes later with two, and a woodpigeon which was rash enough to fly over the Great Meadow at the wrong moment.'

In these immediate post-war years so many rabbits were shot, trapped, netted and snared that early morning trains to London from the affected areas had to be extended in order to carry tens of thousands of rabbits to Smithfield and other markets. Until 1954 meat rationing was still in force, so there was a constant demand for as many rabbits as were available, and I remember one occasion during that September on leave being at Dulverton Station at 5.00 am with a consignment for 'the rabbit train'. If I took rabbits to the local butcher I was paid by weight and have one note of 35½ lbs @ 1/- per lb. Another entry reads: 'Just under an hour after rabbits before dark on the Bracken Bank. Return: 8 for 14 cartridges, most of which were very old and of dubious reliability.' Many of the cartridges had been to Palestine and back, some to Korea, and a few had originated in New Zealand. Most had been damp and the ones that had become swollen had to be discarded. However, when the gun was held straight, those that had dried out appeared to be very adequate.

Throughout the course of my rabbit-shooting experience I became increasingly aware of the vital importance of safety at all times, for there is no shortage of accounts of accidents due to the transgression of approved rules and procedures, let along common sense, in this form of sport. One famous instance recorded in 1884 was a unique case in which a man was shot by a rabbit. A farm labourer, out ferreting, laid his loaded gun down in front of a rabbit burrow and went to listen at the mouth of another burrow a few yards away. While he was thus engaged a rabbit bolted from the first burrow and ran over the gun, discharging it as it did so. Unfortunately, it happened to be pointing directly at the farm labourer, and serious injuries resulted. While such an occurrence could hardly have been foreseen, the sound lesson learned came too late.

Today, thankfully, shooting accidents are fewer than were the case in earlier centuries, and most fathers are conscious of the need to ensure that safety is the foundation of shotgun training for their offspring. It was not until I was confident that my own sons could be absolutely relied on in this regard that we took advantage of the many opportunities we had to shoot rabbits when on holiday in Scotland, where they were far more numerous than at home adjoining Exmoor.

Chapter 21

The Fascination of Salmon

Fishermen as a fraternity have a reputation for embellishing their account of events in which they or others known to them have been involved. Many stories have a ring of truth, while others may lack it in favour of humour or effect. Perhaps the line for anglers to avoid crossing is best determined by personal judgement, and if records have been kept they must become the basis for accurate recollection.

As I began fishing at the age of eight I have had to rely mostly on my memory for the early years, but subsequently I kept at least sporadic records, which include my Junior Members Licence for the season issued on 1 April 1936 by the Derwent Anglers Association, taking 2/6 (12½p) of my pocket money. Further perusal of my fishing records accumulated over the years revealed that the second oldest licence to survive is one dated 9 May 1936, not related to a river in Northumberland but rather to the River Severn. This was issued while I was a pupil at Shrewsbury School, past which the river flows. Mr Pendlebury, a master who was a keen angler, was able and willing to assist boys suffering from piscatorial withdrawal symptoms. He had access to a well-stocked tributary that offered better sport than the main river, and I was one of a number of lucky boys who benefited from his kindness and advice. Most of the time, competitive and recreational rowing dominated activities on the Severn, and although I remember tempting a few trout from it they were, for whatever reason, omitted from my early fishing records.

These opportunities in Shropshire, however, were transient, and most of my early fishing was in Durham or Northumberland, both of which counties had fishing galore suitable for a youngster. A letter written in 1936 to me from a stranger who by coincidence lived in my mother's former family home near Shotley Bridge begins:

> I understand from your sister that you are an enthusiastic fisherman and might be interested to try a small stretch of water on the Allen [a tributary of the Tyne] ... If you are in any doubt as to the boundaries, the woodman, Askew, will explain them to you and will direct you by the right path to the lower part of the water.

He also mentioned that if I liked to accept his invitation I would need the usual Tyne Fishery Board licence, which at 3/6 seemed much more expensive than the Derwent Anglers Association fee.

One thing that I never lacked as a beginner was advice. Within a few years, when parental supervision was no longer considered necessary, I would be dropped off by car at some convenient point of access to Northumberland's River Derwent, with a clear understanding of which bridge downstream I should reach by an appointed time to be collected. This was a major step in my early sporting progress, and as likely as not I would encounter Geordie anglers taking a break from their work. They were invariably friendly and never slow to offer angling advice. One example of this went into my fishing diary, which I had already begun by then: "It's aal a mattor of wat to hoy, wheor ye hoy it, and how ye hoy it." Should I be playing a trout some of the encouragement was unorthodox to put it mildly: "There's ne need for a net, man, Ah just hoy them ower me shoulder."

Such interludes ceased on the outbreak of war in 1939, but were resumed after June 1940. Following our evacuation from France, the 8th Battalion of my Regiment, with which I was serving, was concentrated near Okehampton on the northern fringe of Dartmoor, from where we were granted a week's home leave. On our return to Devon it became clear that an indefinite period for reorganisation, reinforcement and re-equipment lay ahead, so the organization of sports and games became a short-term priority. It did not take long to produce a schedule and timetable, after which officers were from time to time free to follow their own interests. At this stage I noticed that some of the streams flowing down from the moor were close enough to our camp to invite investigation, and I was much encouraged by what I discovered. There were enough trout in evidence to suggest the prospect of good sport, and a helpful resident, who observed my interest, directed me to the local ironmonger, who sold fishing tackle. There, on 17 June 1940, for the sum of 7/6 (37½p) I purchased a small, cheap rod, reel and other essentials, plus a trout licence for use within the Rivers Taw and Torridge Fishery District. Discounting a brief holiday visit to the River Exe near Dulverton in 1936, this was the real beginning of my West Country fishing. This later embraced salmon and continued at intervals, subject to the 'exigencies of the Service', until my retirement from the Army; in fact, the River Exe became the scene of my regular fishing, following my father's purchase in 1954 of a beat including the famous 'Black Pool' and 'The Meeting of the Waters', more prosaically shown on modern maps as 'Junction Pool', where the River Barle joins the Somerset Little Exe to become the Devonshire Exe. My father later handed this fishing over to me, and we enjoyed prolific salmon runs in both spring and autumn until the river was hit by UDN (ulcerative dermal necrosis), from which it has never returned to its former glory. Before UDN one could look down from a rocky vantage point above Black Pool and see salmon lying stacked in tiers. Nowadays we are delighted if we see more than a few fish in the pool at any one time.

During the war and throughout my subsequent military service my fishing was mostly limited to those periods that suited the Army rather than the sport. However, I had two home postings that could not have been better timed from the fishing standpoint. The first was during 1957/8 when I was commanding the Royal Northumberland Fusiliers Training Depot on the outskirts of Newcastle; the second was in the mid-1960s when I took command of the Northumbrian Territorial Army Infantry Brigade, which recruited and trained its members in Northumberland and Cumberland. This posting involved me in a considerable amount of travelling, and on occasions it was necessary for me to spend short periods away from my base in Hexham. Unsurprisingly, there were many opportunities to spend an hour or more on some river bank where I had already been given permission to fish, and I always carried a rod in my vehicle.

These two periods in the North of England included much excellent salmon fishing on the River Tweed, where from 1957 onwards I became familiar with many privately owned beats, the owners of which were among the kindest and most generous lairds I ever met. The beats I fished regularly included North Wark, Upper Carham, the Lees Water, Birgham Dub and Tillmouth Park, and on them I caught, within a few years, more salmon than I have done in all the years since. On five of the seven days fishing I enjoyed on the Tweed between 5 February and 4 March 1958 I caught twenty-five fresh run salmon. Of these fourteen were on one day at Carham, where on a day in February the previous year I had caught nine. In those days there was nothing exceptional about returning to my regiment and enlisting trained and willing hands to deal with any quantity of salmon I might produce. Nor was their consumption limited to the Officers' or Sergeants' Messes; coincidentally, records show it was within the same period that the regiment's recruiting figures exceeded those of any other regiment in the Army!

From a fishing standpoint, however, the landing of some of those fish presented problems, particularly on one memorable occasion in February when the temperature was well below freezing, snow was lying on the river banks, and my rod rings were filling with ice and beginning to hinder the running of the line. In such circumstances the only way to avoid losing any fish that had taken the fly was by moving to and fro with as much speed and agility as was possible along the conveniently open, albeit snowbound, bank. Notwithstanding the practical difficulties, I managed to keep in touch with one fish that, despite iced rod rings, a hesitant, half-frozen reel and snow that limited my movements, was netted by a commendably sure-footed boatman, who later assured me that he had never before seen or heard of anything quite like it. The clearest recollection of another occasion when the low temperature caused problems was in unseasonably cold weather one May, when I was fishing with friends near Ballater, just below where the River Muick runs into the Dee. Not only did I have to clear ice from my rod rings every two or three casts, but my extremities also became extremely cold. When we paused for lunch I took off my waders and allowed my wife to massage my feet to restore the circulation in my toes. This was watched without comment by our ghillie, Sandy Wilson, a delightful, gentle Highlander with a quiet sense of humour; as he left us at the end of the day he remarked, "I'll see ye all in the morning then. I'll be awa' hame now an' tell Mrs Wilson how to warm me frrrozen feet!"

While on the subject of ghillies, who on some large rivers double up as oarsmen, I think it is fitting to mention the dexterity that many of them possess in boat-handling. Certainly on the Tweed, where they are always known as boatmen, I found them to be outstandingly skilful, helpful and friendly. One old hand I have never forgotten, particularly for his remarkable knowledge of salmon lies depending on the height of the river. This enabled him to say, "Two more casts, sir, and if he's where I guess he'll be, you should have him". It was then astonishing how often a fish would take my fly exactly where he had indicated.

The Aberdeenshire Dee was the only other river of comparable magnitude with which I became as familiar as with the Tyne and the Tweed. As well as that occasion near Ballater, I fished regularly with Chips Jewell, who took a beat each year near Aboyne. Then in the 1990s my wife and I began taking two rods in May on the Upper Crathes and Invery water, immediately below Banchory, where we looked forward every season to meeting the other four fishers, who over the years became firm friends. Between us we enjoyed some excellent sport, and many memories have survived. One of these is of a morning when we followed our usual practice, which meant that my wife fished through a promising pool first and I followed her, being able to throw a longer line and cover more water. After a while Sarah, having fished without success, announced that she would walk up into the town to purchase what was needed for our picnic lunch, and she left as I was casting my first fly. Before she was out of earshot she heard the distinctive whistle I used to give to tell her I was into a fish, so she hastened back, donned her waders and arrived at the water's edge with the landing net. Some minutes later she expertly netted a lovely silver fish and waited while I unhooked the fly before setting off again to go shopping. Again came the whistle, and this was repeated three more times in the space of the next two hours. She was eventually able to go shopping, and when we gathered with our friends at the fishing hut for lunch we discovered that the whole episode had been discreetly observed from the opposite bank. One of that group of friends was David Barr, a delightful solicitor from Norfolk, who was also one of the most popular and amusing contributors to Trout & Salmon magazine. Some months later his account (perhaps a little embellished!) appeared in that publication to remind us all of a very entertaining interlude. In those days we were permitted to keep, at our discretion, any fish caught, and these five were all eaten, either fresh or smoked.

Our May fishing at Banchory came in term time, but we used to return in July with our two sons when the summer holidays had begun. The first year we did this I drove up a week early to fish with Chips Jewell, and Sarah followed with the boys the day after term ended. They travelled overnight on the sleeper from Bristol to Edinburgh, had breakfast at the Waverley Hotel and then caught the train to Aberdeen, the entire journey adding considerably to the enjoyment of the holiday for boys aged eight and six. Chips was a friend dating from pre-War Cambridge days, a Scot who had the misfortune to be exiled as a London solicitor and therefore took every possible opportunity of returning to his native land. One of the best salmon I ever caught was with him on the River Hope, where Sarah and I had joined the Jewell family at a fishing lodge perched above the river. Conditions were excellent, which went some way to counteract the aggravation of the midges, and halfway through the week I landed a magnificent 23lb fish.

One year after our family visit to the Dee we drove west and took the ferry to North Uist, where we watched otters swimming among the rocks. We also took a boat out on Loch Maddy, and the most memorable aspect of the good sized fish I managed to land there was the character to whom we took it to be smoked. Having met him and established that he was happy to do the smoking and send the finished product to us at home, I then went to the back of the car to lift out the fish. "No, no, no," came a shout from the smoker as he watched me. He then expounded his theory that to achieve the very best results one should treat a fish gently, with great respect, and proceeded to pick it up and caress it as carefully as if it had been a newborn baby. I do have to admit that the end result, smoked over peat, was among the most delicious smoked salmon I have ever enjoyed.

On the way home from the Outer Hebrides we broke the journey in Dumfriesshire with the idea of reconnoitring the River Nith. We were told at the tackle shop in Thornhill of various access points, and by great good fortune while we were having our picnic lunch at one of them a ghillie appeared. He could not have been friendlier, outlining the possibilities for fishing and even showing us a cottage within walking distance that could be rented by the week. It transpired that he, Bill Kerr, was a retired sergeant from the Parachute Regiment, and my own service in that regiment ensured that we had many memories to share. He became a firm ally of the boys when we returned each July for the next seven years, teaching them how to worm as well as guiding them in fly-fishing. Unfortunately, we never seemed to be there when there was any abundance of fish, but the Nith is a very attractive river to fish, particularly the beats on the Drumlanrig Estate, where Sarah and I took a week several times in October. Beautiful surroundings can go some way to counteract the despondency of not even seeing a fish move, let alone show an interest in one's fly.

Among the sixty-one rivers for which I have a record of having fished there were many contrasts and complexities, but one question determined my preferences: did I instantly feel at ease when actually fishing a river, rather than weighing up its known merits and drawbacks in order to reach a conclusion? Certainly the presence or absence of fish on the bank matters, but how much? Fishermen differ widely in their opinions, and I have learned during well over eighty years of fishing the importance of maintaining a sense of perspective. Most importantly, fishing should be enjoyed, and my outlook is that this cannot be achieved without at least the prospect of landing a fish, though that is not all. Every fisherman will have his or her own ideas on what else is necessary, but from a personal standpoint part of the enjoyment is the prospect of meeting friends, some of whom one may not have seen since the previous season. My wife and I were fortunate enough to count ourselves members of two groups of friends which met annually, one on the Aberdeenshire Dee and the other on the Border Esk, over many seasons. This, and the greeting each year from the ghillies we had come to know, was almost as important as catching fish!

However, it is not the memory of fishing friends, much as we look forward to meeting them again, but rather the glimpses of rivers and countless features associated with them, that can return vividly to me, whether wakeful or half-dreaming at night. Yet by day some mention of a favourite river can bring familiar angling friends to mind as if they were an integral part of it – and so, in a sense, they were.

Chapter 22

Sea Trout and Otters

A mong all the rivers I have fished for salmon there are many that are also renowned for their sea trout; and because salmon are in the main sought by day and sea trout by night, the combination is responsible for limiting the hours of sleep of those of us who wish to pursue both. One of the attractions of fishing is finding oneself on a remote stretch of river, far removed from human habitation, where pleasure can be derived from observing wildlife; and I still regard the five to six miles of the River Coquet between Felton and Weldon Bridge in Northumberland as among the most enchanting. Interestingly, this was not always the case, because throughout the nineteenth century this river was heavily populated with 'bull trout', sometimes known as 'slob' trout, brown trout which leave the river to feed in the estuary. Many thousands were netted annually in the lower reaches and subsequently exported to France. This led to fierce commercial rivalry, and many were the fights between traders and customs officers. However, pollution of the estuary meant that bull trout numbers diminished, and the Coquet resumed its air of tranquillity.

When I was fishing the Coquet before the Second World War, part of the stretch above Felton was privately owned and my enjoyment of it was by invitation, while the remainder was in the hands of the Northumbrian Anglers Federation, of which I became a junior member. So it was here, during my mid-teens, that I became familiar with sea trout and their ways, particularly by night. Indeed, I was one of those fortunate boys whose parents permitted them to fish after dark unaccompanied on rivers they knew well, confident that they were capable of looking after themselves and able to swim out of trouble should the need arise. The vital necessity, however, was familiarity with the river bank or river bed likely to be traversed by night. In such settings I became a nocturnal angling enthusiast and soon gained the necessary confidence to cast a trio of sea trout flies throughout nights when it was too dark to observe them.

In these circumstances, the main purpose behind the periodical examination of one's flies is not so much the need to ensure that they have not become entangled, but to see that they are free of particles of lichen or strands of weed from the river. Otherwise, providing those who have such an opportunity are completely at ease when fishing during the darkest of nights, there can be many advantages and much satisfaction from being on a river shortly before dawn, when movement within the natural world intensifies. Then it is that 'the most noble of fish', as the sea trout is known to many of its admirers, tends to become more active. So in order to ensure that I would be wakeful at this time I often spent a few middle hours of the night making use of an early type of sleeping bag to keep warm under trees close to the river bank. In such a setting one becomes another occupant of the natural world which is generous with its surprises, of which sea trout seem to produce more than their fair share. It is these that can contribute so much to the enjoyment of efforts to outwit them – and eventually get them on to the bank.

A memorable surprise came my way one morning as dawn was breaking and I was sitting against a tree on a bank overlooking the Coquet before starting to fish. Slowly the outline of a roe deer took shape upwind of me, and gradually the gap between us narrowed until I was able to study its features at very close range; but having a rod rather than a gun I was spared the need to shoot the creature, for which I was thankful. Had I been armed I could not have hesitated to kill it, for the damage deer do to young trees is such that most landowners in those parts, and virtually all who own plantations of young trees, regard them as pests. I well remember how as a boy, before I knew better, I failed to react when a roe came past me during a day's pheasant shooting, also in Northumberland, and was taken to task later by my host, whose estate included many young plantations. My excuse for not shooting that roe, which had offered me an easy chance, was the proximity of beaters at the critical moment, but my host was not impressed and suggested that I should somehow have been able to fire a safe shot. As a young guest I knew the importance of accepting such observations without any ifs or buts, even if I had acted in the interests of safety.

My memories of the pleasure I experienced fishing at night on the Coquet as a boy are matched by those of fishing in my seventies and eighties on the Border Esk. My wife and I had the good fortune to be invited by a friend to join a party of fishers on a picturesque stretch of the river just north of Canonbie. We were made so welcome by everyone that we looked forward each year to meeting them again and sharing the cottage that went with the fishing. In the 1990s there was an abundance of sea trout offering excellent night time sport, and even by day it was possible for one of our number to be sent out to catch our supper, which was then expertly barbecued in the garden. Again it was not only the prospect of fishing that provided enjoyment; being on the river bank with the heady scent of honeysuckle and meadowsweet, the silent swoop of an owl over the darkened water and the plaintive call of oystercatchers as dawn was breaking all added to the magic. Unfortunately, the area was one of the most severely affected by foot and mouth disease in 2001, and the amount of disinfectant that seeped into the river had a disastrous effect on the whole ecosystem. For several years very few sea trout were even seen, but thankfully after nearly a decade the balance of the river appears to be restored.

The allure of fishing in beautiful surroundings could not have been illustrated better than at Woodend on the Aberdeenshire Dee, particularly on the captivating Moral Pool. Here, during the years when I drove north from the West Country to fish for salmon by day on a beat at Aboyne or Banchory, I would be able to fish for sea trout at night by virtue of the generosity of the McHardys. One of their regular fishers was an elderly gentleman so wedded to routine that he always called a halt to his fishing every day at precisely 4.00 pm. We sometimes wondered what would have happened had he been into a fish at that time, but history does not relate whether that problem ever arose. What it did mean, however, was that the river was always free in the evening, and I was routinely invited to enjoy this wonderful stretch of water. It was here that I first had an opportunity to try a fly known as 'Katie Jane', designed by a friend and named after his granddaughter. He had always thought of it as a salmon fly, but when he gave me a sample to try out I immediately recognised that it had potential for sea trout. I had several made in different sizes and was delighted to have my judgement confirmed by repeated success, to the mystification of other fishers using some of the conventional patterns of fly who saw my regular entries in the Woodend fishing register.

Today, when I look back on my progress as a young fisherman, I am conscious of the haphazard way in which I gained my experience, for at no stage was I given any systematic family instruction; indeed, my father's sporting interests lay mainly in game shooting though, interestingly, he took to fishing late in life, at times under my tutelage. But for myself, when I was young, I was mainly dependent on two successive gamekeepers, both of whom were themselves largely self-taught. However, another way of looking at this subject is to recognise that nature itself is the supreme teacher for all observant pupils; thus talented naturalists can become interpreters to those who recognise the need to listen and widen their understanding. Within the realm of fishing, anyone seeking guidance has been particularly well served by generations of angling authors who have recorded their experience and advice since the days of Izaak Walton, who died aged ninety in 1683. At some stage the majority of committed anglers find it necessary to take advantage of the remarkable range of fishing publications available to them.

Before long, as a young angler, I began to collect fishing books, of which even then there was a vast choice. In consequence, fishing eventually extended its appeal to me regardless of season, due to my interest in sampling the angling knowledge and views of others. Of this there can be no end, proof of which I am reminded of whenever I visit the Flyfishers' Club in London, which I joined almost sixty years ago. Its collection of nearly 3,000 angling books continues to grow, and there can be no fishable river in the United Kingdom that lacks reference in that library. However, having steadily built up my own modest collection, I have the advantage of being able to browse at leisure, which inevitably leads to the adoption of favourites as well as the discovery of new gems. By this means, many years ago I stumbled upon a book linked with a further experience I had on the River Coquet. This was the close sighting of an otter that was so occupied in its hunt for breakfast that it failed to spot me sitting at a higher level on the same bank. I had never before had the opportunity to watch an otter so close in the wild, and a short while later I was describing it to a knowledgeable friend in Rothbury, further up the river. He was most interested in my story and mentioned an account he had read years before concerning a tame otter from the Coquet that had established quite a reputation. I was able to trace the book in question and found that the story had fascinated all who heard it at the time. I doubt if any local angler of the mid-nineteenth century was more highly respected than William Henderson, who had become recognised as an authority on local lore and legend. In his autobiography, dated 1879, he recounts how Mark Aymsley, a young apprentice from Rothbury, had captured a young otter and adopted it as a pet. They became devoted to each other, and at night the otter, known as Ben, would share his pillow in bed. As time passed Mark took the otter with him when he went fishing, and soon Ben was catching and retrieving trout much faster than his master. But once he had caught about five, and laid them at his master's feet, he would take the next one a short distance away in order to consume it himself.

Not everyone regarded otters in the same light, and at almost the same time Francis Francis, in his book *By Lake and River*, published in 1874, made some interesting proposals:

> There are a great many otters on the Dee and some very large ones are frequently seen … Supposing an otter to require a fish a day, he takes as much as one rod would from the river during the rod-fishing season; only the otter is fishing all the year round, and if there be very many otters, as there are said to be, the wonder is that any salmon are left in the river. I strongly recommend the most stringent measures being adopted to keep them down. If these be not adopted they must speedily make a considerable clearance in the fish. They cannot be hunted in so large a stream, but they may be trapped and shot.

Thankfully, I do not think his recommendation was widely adopted.

Only once did I see an otter myself on the Dee, and that was when I was fishing for salmon late in the evening on a beat at Dinnet. Having made a cast and watched my fly move round with the current I was just about to retrieve it when in the bright moonlight I became aware of an otter swimming upstream towards me. I remained motionless, and he appeared to be quite unaware of me until he was right under my rod, at which point he reared up, audibly spat at me, pirouetted on his tail and then dived so smoothly there was no sign of a splash, just a few bubbles momentarily showing on the surface of the water.

Following the sad decline of otters to a low point in the mid-1980s they have now staged a remarkable recovery, and my own liking for them is rewarded by reports of periodic sightings locally. Indeed, the very day I am writing this I have received word that one was seen this morning in Black Pool on my own stretch of the River Exe. We also know that there has been a travelling dog otter in the area because, although I have only once actually seen him, emerging from a pond on my farm, there have been signs of his presence on other occasions, when he has left the skeleton of a trout on the bank, the skin neatly folded back and the bones picked clean. I take no issue with the loss of a fish now and then, regarding it as part of the balance of nature and an addition to the richness of country life.

Chapter 23

Wildlife in Lapland

In 1976 my wife and I undertook an extensive tour of Northern Scandinavia, the highlight of which was an exploration of Lapland. Because at the time I was involved in National Park administration at home, I had planned a route to take us through several in Finland, Norway and Sweden. As a result of the professional contacts I had already made we found ourselves repeatedly welcomed and assisted throughout our visit.

Our route was destined to take us well north of the Arctic Circle, and, having been warned that August was the only month when it does not snow there, we set off on 24 July in a Range Rover, the new type of Land Rover introduced only five years previously and at that time still a practical and modestly priced vehicle. It was ideally suited to our purpose, and with its rear seat removed we had space for everything we might need during an exacting trip, including fishing rods because, having fished in Scandinavia when visiting in a military capacity, I hoped to have the opportunity of a little trout fishing. We took the night ferry from Felixstowe to Gothenburg and thirty-six hours later were being briefed in the offices of the National Environment Protection Board in Stockholm. We were then taken out for a sumptuous smörgåsbord luncheon, before visiting the Morga Nature Reserve, which covers some 660 hectares and where we learned that there were just over a thousand such nature reserves in Sweden, in addition to their extensive National Parks. That evening we observed from our hotel bedroom window how popular night jogging had become through woodland, with paths illuminated by lamps suspended from trees.

The next day we drove to the 'High Coast', overlooking the Gulf of Bothnia, where we were met by majestic views: coastal fishing villages, little changed since they were built several centuries ago, shared the landscape with farms on the lower slopes and forests above, representing the country's three principal traditional industries. Our journey continued to introduce surprises, including massive accumulations of floating logs in the river basin west of Umeå and the vast dam to produce electric power at Sofors. We also had a briefing on the extensive Vindelfjallen nature reserve, which stretches westwards from our route in central Sweden to a point not far from the border with Norway. We were told that its 'million plus' acres had about twenty-five inhabitants.

On the eighth day of our expedition we crossed the Arctic Circle, within which we would spend most of our time, and arrived at Jokkmokk, a small town where we stayed the night. By now we were beyond any tarmac surfaces and set off on a rough, stony road to cover the eighty miles to Kvikkjokk, meeting only one other car during a journey of several hours. We had already encountered two contrasting species of wildlife to which we soon became accustomed, mosquitoes and reindeer, one familiar and hostile and the other new and relatively friendly. One morning when we awoke in an isolated hut we found a young reindeer asleep under our window. Another great pleasure was observing raptors that are only rare visitors to Britain, such as the gyrfalcon, the flight of which will excite anyone lucky enough to see it. Whether it was exceptional or not we had no means of knowing, but one day a golden eagle descended to around a hundred feet and circled us, as though with curiosity, thereby presenting us with a privileged view. The additional advantage of binoculars revealed its plumage, although I cannot claim to have observed its characteristic, deep-sunk, yellow eyes, which, as Thomas Bewick (1753-1828) observed, 'sparkle with uncommon lustre'.

At Kvikkjokk we were scheduled to leave our car and be flown by helicopter to Lake Virihaure in Padjelanta National Park, which was otherwise accessible only by a three-day walk. However, because the weather was fine and sunny, with perfect visibility, the plan was amended to fly us first right through the middle of the neighbouring mountainous Sarek National Park, considered by many authorities to be Europe's finest and largest. As we approached Sarek, in perfect flying conditions, we were dumbfounded by a vista of unimaginable grandeur and beauty; never before had I seen a landscape to match it, nor have

I done so since. We flew across the centre of its 749 square miles, which bore no visible trace of human hand, and realised that what we were transfixed by was as God and Nature intended. Then we suddenly sensed that we were about to land, though our pilot gave no warning and remained silent throughout. When the rotor stopped he signalled us to follow him in silence and began to stalk towards a low ridge. Still there was no explanation, but clearly there was a surprise to come. As we reached the ridge, he signed that we were to crawl behind him until we were able slowly to peer over it. There in front of us, only about fifteen yards away, was a family of Arctic fox cubs at play. Our pilot turned out to be also a naturalist, with something of the magician about him, for the whole performance was masterly.

Continuing our flight to Padjelanta, we circled low on several occasions to observe elk, which reacted to the helicopter in different ways. One plunged into a lake and submerged for as long as it could hold its breath, before resurfacing and spluttering so much that the water seemed to explode all around it. We landed on the shores of Lake Virihaure, near a log cabin designed for the use of the superintendent on his occasional visits, which would be ours for the following three days, including my birthday. Looking westwards we saw a narrow range of mountains, through which runs the border with Norway, and just beyond it, only some twenty-five miles from where we stood, was the road we would travel on our homeward route.

At the log cabin we were greeted by an experienced mountain guide, who knew the area well and spoke of its characteristics and wildlife with considerable authority. We learned that if we were observant and used our binoculars we might see several species of Europe's rarest fauna, including bear, wolf, lynx and wolverine. The next three days became memorable, as we discovered what a remote and bewitching area Lapland is. Although some weeks had elapsed since the longest day and its almost twenty-four hours of daylight, the nights were still hardly darkening, and the first evening we were collected again by helicopter to be taken, together with a Lapp guide, to the side of a distant mountain, from which we walked a few miles to watch a rare spectacle. This was the annual marking of reindeer calves, following 'the gathering' of the dispersed herd of many hundreds into a large stockade, shown on our map as a Rengarde. This event was characterised by uncertainty due to wind conditions and, perhaps even more so, because of the inclinations of the reindeer, which could be herded after a fashion by Lapps on all-terrain vehicles, but which refused to be hurried. In this vast park of some eight hundred square miles there were around ten thousand reindeer, belonging to about sixty families.

In August there remains enough light throughout the night to read a map, but once the sun has set the Arctic cold reasserts itself with a vengeance and we had a bitter wait for the reindeer as the temperature dropped and we huddled on the tundra with a group of Lapps who had lit a small fire of roots and dry moss. Occasionally the CB radio carried by Bror Läntha, our guide, crackled into life, usually to report a delay in the anticipated time of arrival of the reindeer, and so the hours passed as we became colder and colder. Eventually, our vision of a thousand reindeer being gathered into the stockade below us faded, as our guide looked increasingly often at his watch and then said what could only be taken to mean, "Now we go home". We set off on a seven-mile hike across shallow bogs and snow until we reached a river some hundred yards wide, ice-cold but shallow enough to wade, with Sarah carried on the back of our sure-footed guide. The last two miles were through scrub willow, and almost at the end of our trek we were rewarded with the sight of the snow on the mountains behind us turning a beautiful rose pink as it reflected the sunrise. The whole expedition was unforgettable, even though we had been thwarted in our efforts to see the gathering of the reindeer.

Before we left Lake Virihaure we visited a Lapp settlement where there was a little turf-covered church, resembling a circular beehive surmounted with a wooden cross. All the children appeared invariably cheerful, well-behaved and not at all shy of strangers. Neither were they surprised at the arrival of a seaplane, which was our transport back to Kvikkjokk. There we were reunited with our Range Rover and set off for a brief visit to the Muddas National Park, before we crossed the border into Finland. At the Pallas-Onnastunturi National Park we learned more about the Finnish approach to their visitors. What we refer to as Information Centres they know as Guidance Centres, which suggests a subtle difference. No vehicular access is allowed into the parks, but good provision is made for hikers, including log cabins. Most of these have fireplaces, with the firewood brought in by forest rangers because all trees within the parks are sacrosanct. I was particularly interested to learn of the importance they attached to noise suppression within their national parks and wished that we, too, had the same outlook. In my view, it should be included in our own Country Code.

The farther we travelled north, the starker and more impressive the scenery became, coupled with such features as the old Lapp fishing village of Kalakentät, which was known as one of the seven wonders of Finland. Yet most of northern Finland is sparsely populated, and it was uplifting to travel for hours on almost deserted roads through a landscape containing thousands of lakes. From time to time we parked the car and took to our feet for exercise, and on one occasion we rounded a corner to find a splendid reindeer stag in our path, looking the other way. We froze, and it was at least half a minute before he got wind of us and moved back into cover, but not before I had his photograph. At the end of each day during our visit there was accommodation available, varying from simple huts to small hotels, and the people, though often reserved at first, soon became friendly and helpful.

The most easterly stop on our travels, and almost the most northerly, was at Inari, where we spent a night and looked across a lake studded with islands to the border with the USSR, only thirty miles away. The following day we drove to Lemmenjoki, Finland's largest national park, where we found ourselves in the hands of an exceptionally competent and experienced boatman, who took us through a series of interconnected lakes for some 15 miles in a long, thin, Lapp boat, powered by an outboard motor. We landed at intervals to view various features, including a magnificent cascade, and whenever a watercourse became too shallow we were invited to walk alongside while our guide pulled the boat into deeper water. At the limit of its range we left the boat and walked for some miles up a long ascent into fine, virgin forest containing pine trees, some of which were over five hundred years old. On one of the walks on our return journey we met Matti Flink, one of the few gold-washers to be found in the only two areas in Finland where this is possible. He was a courteous man, who spoke enough English to answer our questions as we watched him, fascinated, for nearly an hour. It was a skilful performance as he swirled just enough water to fill his large, shallow pan with its contents of gravel and sediment taken from a small stream that looked just like any other, but had its secrets. Before we left he asked if I would like to try my hand. It was, of course, much harder than it looked when done by an expert, but in a while I was rewarded with a few small flakes of gold. These he gave to me in a tiny, clear glass bottle with a screw top, which had a magnifying glass let into it, thereby exaggerating the extent of my achievement. He then presented Sarah with a small, uncut, sapphire. As was so often the case, we were bowled over by the combination of charm and generosity. Then it was time to retrace our steps to the boat, which took us part of the way to the local warden's house, where we were offered coffee before we returned to our cabin for the night, finding all the facilities we needed to make a good meal from the supplies we carried.

The sun was shining brilliantly by the time we rose to continue our journey north, eventually crossing the border into Norway, where the first of the fjords came into sight, with the Arctic Ocean now on our right. Much of the next day we spent in the Øvre Dividalen National Park, which was surrounded by a three-mile exclusion zone for cars. Whatever the reason, whether it was to exclude fumes or people, or both, it added six miles of walking to the distance we covered inside the park. Either way, it served its purpose admirably because, apart from one or two fishermen, we never met a soul as in solitude we appreciated the magnificent mountain scenery. The following night we spent in Narvik, rising at 5.30 am to catch the first train to the Abisco National Park, one of several created in 1909 and much frequented by skiers. A ski-lift took us up to 3,000 feet to admire the view, before we walked back down. We then visited the cemetery in Narvik where, in a separate section, lie the graves of many British servicemen who lost their lives during the battles of Narvik in 1940 and in later engagements. Driving a further 150 miles south, we saw the mountainous Rago National Park to the east, which we had previously admired from the opposite side when it was only 25 miles from us, over the lake in Padjelanta. In the meantime, those 25 miles had become 1,060 as we took the shortest road to reach the other side. Such limitations in the choice of routes contributed much to the character of a holiday we still regard as out of the ordinary, with unforgettable memories.

After Rago, we had four days in which to wend our way southwards, visiting another three national parks. At the Børgefell National Park we met three Norwegian youths and discovered that, as well as vehicles being excluded, dogs were not permitted unless they were working. They had with them a splendid 'pack-dog', who answered to the name of 'Boy' and wore a harness with two panniers in which he carried their provisions as well as his own, up to a weight of fifteen kilos. The last park we visited was Rondane, and here for the first time encountered quite a number of other visitors. When we rejoined the main highway to Oslo we found settlements increasingly close together and had to get used to meeting other vehicles. The capital itself proved to be quite a navigational test, because of its multitude of one-way streets. We spent a full day there before our midnight sailing to Newcastle and were glad to have reconnoitred our way to the docks before night fell. In fact, after several false turns, we resorted to asking the occupants of a Police Traffic Control car for their help. They laid out our street map on the roof of their vehicle and even then had to discard the first two routes they started to suggest, finding themselves baulked by the one-way system. However, their final solution seemed to be clear, and we later made our way to the SS *Bolero* without any trouble. After our wonderful travels even the voyage home was not without interest, as we were able to go ashore for a few hours at Kristiansand and then, in the North Sea, were able to see low rain clouds glowing with the reflected light of burning gas from oil rigs.

Chapter 24

Sporting Interludes in Germany

M y recollections of game shooting in Germany belong to several distinct periods, the first of which was in the spring of 1945, as the war was drawing to its close in Western Europe. The Third Infantry Division was withdrawn from the River Maas in order to prepare for the crossing of the Rhine and the fighting that lay ahead, including that in the Reichswald Forest. As our occupation extended in Germany we continued to confiscate all privately owned firearms for immediate destruction, and because speed was essential the units with this responsibility were often those furthest forward. The Bürgermeister (mayors) were summoned and made responsible for ensuring that all civilian weapons were handed in to specified collection points within a matter of hours. With typical German efficiency this was complied with, then all the weapons were laid out on a road and run over by tanks or tracked carriers. In this way thousands of rifles and shotguns, including some of the highest quality, were destroyed, and I sometimes wondered how I would have felt if our positions had been reversed. One old gentleman, who spoke fair English, came up to me with a shotgun which he obviously cherished; with tears in his eyes he implored me to take it and save it from destruction. After he had explained what it meant to him I found myself for the first and only time in my service 'colluding with the enemy', not because I admired his gun but because I understood his feelings. The gun never took the place in my affections of 'Uncle Kit', but it gave some sterling service, because in the gaps between periods of intense operational activity there were still opportunities for sport to augment our rations.

None was more significant than that mentioned in my letter home dated 10 March 1945. 'I am now allowed to say that we are in Germany' was followed by such news as was acceptable to the censor. Then, as was often the case, the rest of my letter was of a sporting nature. Although we were well into March, wartime conditions took no account of close seasons, and these were stretched in moderation according to conscience. On one day three of us fitted in a morning duck flight during which we shot two mallard, one teal, one pheasant, two rabbits, two woodpigeons and a roe deer. I also noted that cartridges were getting very low, and I had got down to my last twenty-five before someone produced four hundred and fifty that had been confiscated from a local German who was no longer permitted to possess them.

On 8 May the Second World War in Europe came to an end, and for some weeks we were so involved with humanitarian tasks in Germany that time for any form of sport or recreation was extremely limited. Within days of the armistice we found ourselves on numerous occasions having to defend German families against bands of Polish and Russian ex-prisoners of war, who were determined to seek revenge for years of oppression while suffering in confinement or under occupation. Often all that was required to ensure the maintenance of law and order was the presence of a detachment of British troops, because we were regarded not only as the victors but also as the rescuers of thousands of our allies whose countries had been overrun. Our military role suddenly changed from active service to peacekeeping, and it took longer than most of us had anticipated to broaden our outlook and deal with the great range of humanitarian responsibilities then facing us. Early in the process we were confronted by the horrors awaiting us in what had become the British Zone of Germany. In the course of our advance into the interior of Germany our forces came across ghastly Nazi prison camps and execution centres, where the actual situation turned out to be far worse even than the reports that preceded their revelation suggested. It is important not to overlook this horrific aspect, even in a sporting account; that might otherwise suggest a reprehensible lack of concern towards one of the worst examples of inhumanity in modern times. In the circumstances, it was all the more commendable how our troops came to terms with every situation they encountered and committed themselves with fortitude to tackle them.

It came as something of a surprise, as well as a relief, to witness the arrival of thousands of qualified British aid workers, fully equipped and trained to take on their share of Europe's post-war problems.

It was in consequence of the required precautions against sometimes appalling, though understandable, revenge attacks, that I found myself spending much of my time visiting widespread detachments of my squadron; and in the course of my rounds it became a frequent bonus to be told of sightings of game and wildfowl. Usually such information came from within the squadron, but before long some of the German farmers whose families and stock we had helped to protect, having seen me previously setting out with a shotgun or returning from some sporting reconnaissance, began, by way of appreciation, to offer me suggestions on areas where I might enjoy further sport. In those early months it was not approved for the British to converse with Germans other than in connection with residual problems linked with the war and its aftermath; but the situation slowly changed, and gradually the 'non-fraternisation' rule was eased.

However, relations were still cool during my next interlude in Germany, when I spent most of 1949 as a company commander in the 1st Battalion the Parachute Regiment, which was stationed on the outskirts of Brunswick in northern Germany. There we occupied a former German army cavalry barracks, in the stables of which were some thirty horses. Most of them were in excellent condition and still thriving under the management of their rather formidable and highly experienced German ex-cavalry warrant officer, by then employed and paid by our battalion. So committed was he to the care of the horses that he hardly seemed to notice that they no longer belonged to the Third Reich, and he continued to expect that all who wished to ride them should measure up to his high standards. Nobody ever disillusioned him about any of these niceties, and our soldiers who acted as grooms were chosen with some regard for their tact. Initially he had difficulty in adjusting to the light-hearted approach of equestrian parachutists towards his venerable profession, but as the relationship developed the red berets began to show something akin to respect for him, while he in turn almost learned to smile again. Fortunately, one of our subalterns was an accomplished horseman and was duly made responsible for stable management. One of his early concerns was to rename the horses, and all the existing name boards bearing German names were taken down to be repainted with English ones, mostly chosen with care. At this stage a battalion exercise intervened, from which we returned to find all the name boards returned to their appointed stalls, bearing their new names. As company commander I had 'first call' on a handsome horse, which according to the smart board painted in airborne colours on his stall was now called 'Mistry'. For a while the origin of this name remained a mystery, until it dawned on me that some parachutists, including junior officers, have their spelling problems.

The 1st Battalion the Parachute Regiment was part of 16th Parachute Brigade Group, and our priority was to ensure an advanced state of operational readiness, so the intensity of training within the Rhine Army was maintained at a high level. However, within such spare time as remained, our physically energetic commanding officer favoured the pursuit of the maximum number of sporting activities. These included rugby, soccer, cross-country running, athletics, boxing, swimming, rifle shooting, skiing and riding. Nevertheless, the enjoyment of field sports within the Rhine Army, even if sometimes limited in availability among so many enthusiasts, was regarded as a major attraction. As the lives of German sportsmen slowly returned towards pre-war conditions, private land ownership was once again respected, and it was quite remarkable how despite, as a nation, having lost in the region of 3,500,000 people killed or missing, within a few years they recovered their traditional sporting outlook.

Against this background it was gratifying to me some years later, when I returned to Germany in 1963, to find that relations had ameliorated to conditions we came to regard as normal. By then we had effectively become allies during the Cold War and, while the latter imposed its own restrictions, there were no longer, in either a diplomatic or sporting sense, any significant differences between us in outlook. It so happened that I was serving further afield during much of this transitional period, so I was surprised to find the extent to which British and German sportsmen had combined under their NATO umbrella and some of my most congenial sporting memories date back to this time. It was then, by invitation and common interest, that we found ourselves sharing the sport available to those equipped with shotguns and mindful of the attractions of true sportsmanship.

My previous shooting in Germany had been mostly of a solitary nature, but now I was comprehensively introduced to shooting for sport as conducted by the Germans. Professionalism is, of course, regarded as one of their characteristics, and it was to be found as much in the shooting field as in any of their other activities. Absent were the relaxed attitudes which typified so many of the English shoots I knew; however, where, in my view the Germans had established an indisputable lead over us at that time was in the routine which followed the conclusion of an enjoyable day's shooting. In my experience in England there were apt to be three options: the first consisted of thanks to the host, tips to the keepers, a quick word of farewell to the other guns, then into the car and away. The second was the substitution of shooting footwear for clean shoes and into the host's house for tea before departure. The third was to be invited in for a meal, mainly for the benefit of those with a journey ahead of them, though some might be house guests staying overnight. But not since the days of Jorrocks and his friends, as described by Surtees (1805-64) had British sportsmen enjoyed such entertaining sequels to their sporting activities as in Germany.

The contrast with a day's sport in Germany could hardly have been greater, because there the end of the shooting was still only half-time; and, reminiscent of duck shooting in Manitoba, ahead there lay an extended meal, including much beer and entertainment, ending with music and hearty singing. To many British sportsmen this did not come naturally, though all they needed was a brief conversion course in Bavaria, following which they realised that guests were not only invited in order to enjoy themselves, but also to contribute to the jollity of such occasions. Sadly, it was difficult to visualize any noteworthy change of sporting routine in this regard at home, although here there can be merit in abundance in other respects, and where humour is concerned there can be no end to the recollections that most sportsmen treasure. One of mine originated in the wake of a major NATO exercise in 1949, at the end of which the 1st Battalion the Parachute Regiment was located not far from Luxembourg.

At that time I was commanding 'C' Company, and following some months of rigorous training we had reached the climax of what was regarded as one of the largest-scale exercises of the post-War era, with British, American, French and German participation. In the event, nothing was lacking, while the realism and fervour were such that in the closing stages the umpires were at full stretch in their efforts to maintain control. It was a highly demanding exercise, and in the eyes of the contestants national honour was at stake throughout, though happily good discipline prevailed. Nevertheless, as can be the case on such occasions, it is the incidents rather than the main event that survive with clarity in the memory, and so it proved as Exercise 'Runflat' reached its conclusion in the battle of Thalfang, east of Luxembourg. From there we had several hours of daylight in which to disperse into sheltered, isolated areas to spend the night.

My company quartermaster sergeant was Paddy Byrne, a splendid Irishman who had won the Military Medal for gallantry on active service with the Irish Guards before he re-enlisted with the Parachute Regiment after the War. He was an exceptionally fine soldier, with the bonuses of an ability to raise morale whenever the need arose and a never-failing sense of humour. On this occasion he excelled himself by finding a delightful secluded area in which 'C' Company could relax and bivouac. Then came a surprise that contributed much to the enjoyment of the evening, for early in the proceedings, as dusk was deepening, one of our trucks arrived with more beer on board than could reasonably have been hoped for. This was probably the moment when most of those present recognised the potential of the night ahead of them, and thereafter the pace never slackened. All the ingredients were present for a grand party in the open air on a balmy night, with everyone fully relaxed. Yet nobody, apart from Paddy and those directly involved, could have foreseen the climax that was heralded by an indeterminate disturbance in the background, from where a small group from the company was approaching purposefully. There were noises off-stage that sounded like the protestations of a very disgruntled pig, and before long a large sow was half pulled and half pushed past those of us spectating. Then the pig suddenly stopped protesting, and normal conversation was resumed. More beer, with hearty singing, assisted the time to pass, and in due course a pork supper of impressive proportions silenced the singing and provided the seal to a memorable occasion. Episodes such as this contribute to the spice of life.

Chapter 25

The Unique Cresta Run

By the time I went to the Swiss resort of St Moritz in January 1955 as a member of the Army Ski Association I had already been introduced to skiing a few years previously in the Harz Mountains of Northern Germany. There, despite the obvious potential, the existing facilities were still limited, and it was through going to ski on the beautifully managed slopes at St Moritz that I became addicted to riding the Cresta Run. Had I at the time been familiar with the Lonsdale Library volume on Winter Sports, published in 1930, I might have experienced earlier tremors of interest after reading its chapter on tobogganing. However, it still reads as well today as it must have done when it first appeared, and in the meantime winter sports have grown in popularity wherever demand and conditions have favoured them.

Back in 1955 in St Moritz, as I was returning to my hotel after a morning on the ski slopes, I passed close enough to the finish of the Cresta Run to gain an impression of the speed reached by participants, always referred to as 'riders' in the same way that Cresta toboggans are always 'skeletons'. No one could fail to be impressed, and I took an early opportunity, in one of the Kulm Hotel bars, to raise the subject of their sport with two Cresta enthusiasts, although I was already in my mid-thirties, which some might consider rather old to take up the sport. They were no doubt used to people expressing a passing interest, but the outcome of our discussion was an invitation to meet them at eight o'clock the following morning in the old hut at Junction beside the Run. Perhaps they were testing me, but it was a moment of commitment and second thoughts would have been out of the question.

The first lesson for all beginners on the Run is to grasp the importance of understanding the risks. These are part and parcel of its trials as well as its enjoyment, for if the rules and guidelines for safe riding are not observed disaster is inevitable. This can follow inaction as surely as actual errors, so beginners have to think and act positively according to the instructions they have received. I still have my copy of the pocket-size 1957 edition of 'Hints to Riders on the Cresta', which contains sixteen pages of invaluable guidance. Section 6 covers 'Points to be specially remembered', the tenth and last of which advises: 'To ride well is not easy. It takes time and study. There is no short cut. All attempts at this lead to the hospital.'

I cannot now recall whether that first morning I had a hearty breakfast to set me up for the day, but I do remember that I was fired with enthusiasm. My mentors kitted me out with the necessary equipment, a helmet and goggles, knee pads, elbow pads, thick gloves with metal hand-guards and boots with jagged metal 'rakes' riveted to the toe-caps. From a vantage point I watched several experienced riders go down and then was taken to 'Stream Corner', about two thirds of the way down the Run, from which all beginners had to start. I was told that nobody minded how slowly a beginner took his first ride, because the Run was not harmed by a rider raking to reduce speed and it was more important to get to the bottom than to risk a fall. As a novice I was not permitted to take a running start, so after checking that the sliding seat was working freely, I took the skeleton on to the Run, where it was restrained from slipping away by the judiciously placed foot of one of the small maintenance gang. As soon as I was 'comfortably' positioned I gave the signal and was away down what is now known as the Bledisloe Straight. I must have gone very carefully, but it was a matter of seconds before I was over the Cresta Leap and safely down at the Finish, exhilarated and impatient for another turn. It had been just one ride down only a third of the Run, but I was already enthralled.

As the first specialist toboggan run in Switzerland, the Cresta owes its origins to the competitive spirit in 1884 of the Outdoor Amusements Committee of the Kulm Hotel in St Moritz. A year or two earlier, Davos had hosted an International Race down the Klosters Road, and the members of the committee decided to build a Run and invite Davosers to come and compete with St Moritzers. There is a steep gully between St Moritz and the village of Celerina, passing the Cresta hamlet, and this was considered a suitable basis on which to construct an ice-packed run, supervised by two members of the committee, including Major W. H. Bulpett of the British Army. The first 'Grand National' race took place on 21 February 1885, and the whole enterprise was greeted with such enthusiasm that the course was then constructed every year as soon as sufficient snow had fallen, continual improvements being made from year to year largely at the instigation of Major Bulpett. He also invented the metal skeleton toboggan, ridden head-first, which soon replaced the old wooden toboggans, and his influence through the early years may explain how the British relationship with the Cresta developed and prospered with the active support of our armed forces, which through successive generations have contributed to the Club's traditions – as strong today as in former times.

The length of the Run is approximately three-quarters of a mile, over which its course descends 514 feet at an average gradient of 1 in 7.7, with the steepest slope being 1 in 2.8. There are some fifteen named features, including magnificent bends known as 'banks', and spectacular drops, on the last of which – 'Cresta Leap' – speeds in the region of 80 mph are reached by the fastest riders as they approach the finish. Early in its development, before the end of the nineteenth century, some large rocks were blown up and a few permanent earthworks constructed, but since then the Run has been rebuilt every year, except during the two World Wars, by a group of experienced local men led by a highly committed foreman, who supervises the conversion of packed snow into ice, following the natural features of the hillside. Animated discussions take place each season among aficionados as to the relative ease or difficulty of the Run, but I would say that usually only the most experienced riders can detect the minor differences on individual banks. There was one year when a directive had to go out in mid-season to the effect that because of the 'more forgiving' nature of Shuttlecock, less experienced riders who were not used to surviving that bank at speed *must* remember to rake hard as soon as they passed the Finish, because too many were failing to stop before reaching the barrier at the end. Shuttlecock is perhaps the most notorious of the banks, at which even some of the most expert riders can find themselves flying over the top and landing in a bed of snow and scattered straw. The result can be painful, but there is the consolation of being entitled to wear the Shuttlecock Tie and attend the annual Shuttlecock Dinner.

My introduction to the Cresta in 1955 took place towards the end of my holiday in St Moritz, and I was able only to participate on a couple more mornings before I had to return to the Army Staff College at Camberley, where I was an instructor. However, there was no doubt in my mind where I would be heading for my next winter sports break, and January 1956 found me back in St Moritz, determined to ride the Cresta as often as possible. I became a full member of the St Moritz Tobogganing Club and only regretted that I was not in a position to spend the entire season there, although as it happened there was a dramatic paucity of snow in the Engadine that year. The top third of the Run was never opened, and the remainder, from Junction, was only achieved through the determined efforts of a large gang of workmen, moving what little snow there was in the vicinity and watering it to provide the requisite icy surface. There were no snow machines in those days, of course. However, that did not deter me from returning in 1957, when I felt very honoured to be invited to become a Life Member of the Club. Conditions were good, and I improved my technique sufficiently to be invited to compete in the Heaton Gold Cup on 18 and 19 January, quite satisfied at finishing twelfth and only two seconds slower than the legendary Nino Bibbia.

I referred earlier to 'the entire season', but even in the best of years that amounts to only about ten weeks, from just after Christmas to the end of February. Sufficient snow must have fallen and the temperature must remain low enough for the ice not to soften, which is also why riding only takes place during the morning, between 8.00 am and noon. In the 1950s there were some people lucky enough to be able to spend as long as they wished at the resort, but those of us in the Armed Services had to make the best possible use of our annual leave allocation, and anyone good enough to take part in the Inter-Service Championship would try to have at least two weeks of training rides before the competitions. In 1958 I arrived in St Moritz on 3 January, having spent twenty-four hours travelling from Newcastle after Christmas and the New Year at home, and three days later wrote a letter full of enthusiasm to my parents:

> I got here on Friday night and rode on the Cresta on Saturday morning
> – three courses. I was surprised to find myself in very much better form
> than I had expected or even hoped and on Sunday broke my own record
> by nearly a second which was a fantastic development. Saturday was a

practice but was regarded as a qualification for the Calisch Grischun Cup, one of the International Trophies, which was to be competed for the following day. I got a nomination and was very gratified to come 6th of the 30 competitors and 2nd of the British entries.

Today was another practice day and remarkable for the number of riders who turned up for it – 53, which I am told is a record. Again I was surprised to find I had the best time of the day, although it had snowed during the night and conditions were slower than yesterday – admittedly all the snow is swept off the ice, but the atmosphere has the effect of taking half a second or so off one's time.

On the 14th and 15th we have the Inter Services Competition which is an annual event between the Army, Navy and Air Force. Teams of 6 compete over 2 days and the best 4 of each team count. I have been asked to represent the Army and look forward to the competition which is usually close and always bitterly contested. This year will be more skin and hair than ever as Prince Philip has presented a new trophy for it and each service is anxious to win it for its first year. Last year the Army won the event, 1956 the Navy and 1955 the RAF, so you can see how evenly the teams are matched.

When it came to the event, where the winning team is that with the lowest aggregate time for four riders over six courses from Junction during the two days, the Army did manage to win the Prince Philip Challenge Trophy, by half a second from the RAF (1,122.7 seconds to 1,123.2 seconds). We were also competing for the Lord Trenchard Trophy, which goes to the individual rider with the fastest aggregate time over the six courses, and the Auty Speed Cup for the single fastest time. Looking back in the Club's Annual Report for that season I was delighted to be reminded that, 'On his first course Wilson clocked a superb 45.6 to win the Auty Speed Cup for the fastest time in the Services Events. His subsequent 46.1 and 46.3 placed him second in the Lord Trenchard Trophy with an average speed for the six courses of the race of less than two-tenths of a second per run behind the great Mitchell.' Two days later came the Heaton Gold Cup again, and this year I was able to improve my final position from twelfth to third place, only beaten by Nino Bibbia and Colin Mitchell.

While the instructions in the Club's 'Hints to Riders' are eminently practical and straightforward, some notes produced for the Army Ski Association were more light-hearted. One paragraph reads : 'A lot of people wonder what type of man rides the Cresta. Basically he should enjoy skiing, drinking or both, otherwise the afternoons can be dull. Preferably he should not be an expert at either of those sports. An expert skier has little time for practice and a skilled drinker may well be incapable of riding the next day.' Indeed, although my first visit to St Moritz had been to ski, when I wrote home in 1958 I mentioned that, 'So far I have only been on my skis twice although conditions have been excellent. My big worry is not to break or strain anything which will interfere with my Cresta riding.' It was during this period that I was able to assist the Club through the discreet encouragement of suitable entrants, including some of the post-Sandhurst generation of young officers, who would in time play their part in maintaining an exceptional and worthwhile sporting tradition.

Many of the most committed riders had their own 'skeleton', which would be stored at St Moritz from one season to the next. The steel skeleton, with its misnamed sliding 'seat' which supports the rider's chest and takes the weight of his body, is the product of simple but sound engineering, and its lack of friction when in use, almost regardless of the rider's weight, is the main secret of its success. I was extremely fortunate, just before my second visit, to be put in touch with the Hon Ben Bathurst QC, who had reluctantly decided that common sense should prevail and was therefore looking to dispose of his skeleton. I had a charming letter of advice, written from his chambers in Lincoln's Inn, acknowledging the £10 and 25 Swiss francs that he had suggested would be a suitable reimbursement and ending: 'So glad to hear you have "caught the disease". I have been suffering from it for over 30 years.' I wish that I had been able to indulge for thirty years, but sadly, after those four consecutive years in the 1950s and a fleeting visit in January 1960, when adverse conditions led to the cancellation of the Inter-Services race, my army postings meant I was not free to head for St Moritz; and if I did have a few days available at that time of year my other passion, for wildfowling, took me to Holy Island or the Solway Firth. However, in 1976, when I had retired from the army, my wife and I spent a month visiting some of the National Parks in Switzerland, Italy and France, and our travels took us through St Moritz. I was able to pick out the route of the Run from various permanent features and we walked most of its course. Even on a sunny day in August there was a slight rush of adrenalin as I contemplated the gradients at Church Leap near the top and Cresta Leap towards the finish. Paul Gallico, a frequent rider in the 1950s, walked it himself when there was still snow on the ground and wrote an account in a letter to Lord Brabazon, dated 14 March 1956:

> The other day, fed up with my own prose, I went for a stroll on a sunny afternoon and walked down the Cresta from Junction to the top of Finishing Bank. I had never done this. There had been a light snow the night before so that one could do the entire trip on foot inside the banks. What a catalogue of new terrors I have filed away for myself to draw upon next year ... I felt lonely and nostalgic at the end of the walk and wished there were armoured and helmeted figures with whom to share the march back up the hill and to discuss once more just what idiocy I had perpetrated where that had shattered my dreams of cleaving a few fractions of seconds from that miserly old Father time. And I felt more than ever how very unique and wonderful was the Cresta ...

If I had feared in 1976 that I had hung up my Cresta boots forever I had a pleasant surprise coming. In 1997 the Army Winter Sports Association held its 50th Anniversary meeting in St Moritz. Having been a member of the Army Cresta team in 1958 and Chairman of the Army Ski Association Bob and Cresta Committee between 1969 and 1971, I was invited to attend – with the idea, I imagine, that I would be an interested spectator. Sarah and I were not able to arrive in St Moritz in time to watch the Inter-Services race (which was actually won by the Navy), but I noticed on the schedule that there were still several training days before the Army race. I had been skiing with Sarah and our sons as recently as 1993, and my sensible doctor at home passed me fit for winter sports – did I perhaps fail to mention riding the Cresta? So, the morning after our arrival, I went along to the Clubhouse where the Club Secretary, the redoubtable Lieutenant Colonel Digby Willoughby, was delighted to introduce me to a splendid young Scots Guards officer who had taken a bruising tumble the previous day. He was therefore 'off games' for a few days and was very happy to lend me his kit. It might have been that conditions were tricky, but when I had been briefed and was ready to set off from Junction my departure was momentarily delayed because the rider in front of me had a fall. This might have been disconcerting, but as he got to his feet and gave the signal to the Tower that he was unharmed, Digby gave me the all-clear to set off. I successfully pitched myself forward into the correct position on my skeleton, and immediately the thrill returned. In no time I was at the Finish and hopped on to the Camion for a lift back to Junction to get into the queue for another turn. That first ride had taken me half as long again as my winning time in 1958, but after a few more practice runs I was able to improve by more than fifteen seconds. Sarah knew I had been planning to take part in the Retired Officers' race, but I think she was unaware I had been told that was nonsense because I was eligible for the proper Army Championship, albeit the race from Junction rather than the one from Top. There were more than thirty other competitors and all but two of them had handicaps ranging from one to eight seconds, but when I raised the subject with Digby he replied: "Handicap? No, dear boy. You may be rising 78 but you were scratch in 1958 and scratch you remain." Nevertheless, I managed to complete all three courses, improving each time, and finished halfway down the field, my best time of 55.18 seconds being only 7 seconds slower than the winner.

After that wonderful experience I did have to concede that my Cresta days were over, but I still maintain that I shall never be persuaded there is a more thrilling sensation than riding headfirst downhill at 80 mph with one's face only inches from the icy surface, adjusting one's line with the merest inclination of the head and always being aware that even going fractionally too fast will end in disaster. And blended with the high level of excitement that the Cresta Run generates there is no shortage of humour. Some accounts in circulation are no doubt apocryphal, but most have an element of truth. One of my favourites is an account by R. C. Todhunter that appeared in the Annual Report for 1956-7, concerning a horse that found its way on to the run a short distance below Top:

No one knows how he did it. Perhaps he was out for a Sunday morning stroll, but, whatever the cause, he was off down the run in a flash. Wisely he sat down, and considering the speed he gathered down 'Church Leap', all the experts agreed that he took the first three banks like a champion. As he tore through 'Junction', emitting a slight trail of smoke, he looked around him, puzzled but not disturbed. Unfortunately he failed to pay attention to the loud cries of "Rake" from either bank as he tore into 'Rise', which he negotiated safely. Alas, inexperience then betrayed him, and for the first time he looked perturbed, as well he might. He failed to take 'Battledore' early enough, and hitting 'Shuttlecock' with a grunt of alarm, he went soaring out. He was later led into the Shuttlecock Dinner covered in medals.

On what better note could I conclude my story of those far-off happy days on the incomparable Cresta Run, the unequalled sport for those 'sound in body and wanting in mind'?

Chapter 26

The Six-Mile Free Fall Parachute Drop

When writing about free fall parachuting it is necessary to distinguish between military and sporting procedures, for they can differ considerably. In the Army they exist in parallel, but even in the Parachute Regiment only a proportion of soldiers take it up recreationally. Over the last fifty years immense advances have been made in equipment and clothing, but to give an idea of what is involved in the technique of free falling I think I can do no better than quote an article I wrote in 1963, at a time when I was involved in a considerable amount of parachuting:

> In free falling the parachutist is equipped with main and reserve parachutes as for conventional parachuting, but instead of the main canopy being deployed for him by static line as he leaves the aircraft, he falls free for a predetermined time or distance before he opens his parachute by pulling the handle of his ripcord. The time of his drop can be recorded by a stop watch and the distance by an altimeter, both of which are normally mounted on a small panel fixed to the top of his reserve parachute.
>
> After leaving an aircraft the parachutist increases his vertical speed until, after approximately 12 seconds, he reaches terminal velocity (about 120 mph in a flat stable position). Owing to the speed of his descent it is necessary for him to open his parachute higher than the conventional static-line parachutist in order to have a few seconds in hand to use his

reserve in an emergency. For this reason the opening height for free fallers is normally fixed at 2,000 feet. After reaching terminal velocity he will take about 5 seconds to fall 1,000 feet; thus a drop from 12,000 feet will involve about 60 seconds in free fall.

My initial introduction to conventional parachuting had been when I was posted from the Reconnaissance Regiment of the 3rd Infantry Division to 6th Airborne Division in July 1945 and returned from Palestine the following January to attend a standard RAF static-line course at No. 1 Parachute Training Centre at Ringway. The following three years gave me opportunities for a limited number of standard jumps, but my introduction to free fall parachuting did not take place for more than ten years, by which time I had taken command of 22nd Special Air Service Regiment. I had been with them about six months when, in May 1960, a team of free fall parachutists from the US 10th Special Forces Group stationed in Germany came to Hereford for a friendly competition against our own recently formed free fall parachute club, the forerunner of the 'SAS Skydivers'. The Americans had donated a silver cup, which they predictably won, and I was asked to present it to the winning team. Having done so, I assumed that proceedings were over, and was somewhat taken by surprise when their Master Sergeant reappeared carrying a spare parachute, which he offered to me with the invitation to jump with them. I was about to thank him, while explaining that as I had no personal experience of free fall parachuting I was unqualified to accept his offer, when I intercepted a wink between him and members of my team and realised that it was a put-up job. There is no means of knowing whether I would have taken up free fall parachuting in due course anyway, but my team little realised that their challenge was to initiate me into a sport that became a major interest, resulting in my captaining the British Free Fall Parachute team and being invited to be Chairman of the civilian British Parachute Association between 1962 and 1965. That first jump with the Americans, from a mere 2,800 feet, just whetted the appetite.

Throughout the post-war decades the Army and Royal Air Force had both contributed towards the research and development of parachuting, although, within the limits of high altitude parachuting, the Army took the lead in specialist research into what was known as HALO parachuting (High Altitude Low Opening) as a means of inserting small numbers of

Special Forces into situations requiring clandestine entry. It so happened that it was while I was commanding 22 SAS that our future employment came under review in order to categorize priorities in the research of roles, organisation, equipment and training. The Cold War of that era also created its own challenges, and we found ourselves consulting records of previous strategies, including those of the Special Operations Executive during the Second World War. It also behoved us to establish what subsequent progress, if any, had been made during the intervening years. However, most wartime contributors had dispersed, and there were few organisations able to assist, so a complete reassessment became necessary.

At an early stage a stroke of good fortune came my way while I was visiting the Farnborough Air Show of 1961. At the forefront of my mind was an awareness of the lack of any suitable transport aircraft for the future use of our parachute troops. The famous wartime Dakota by then had its limitations and, notwithstanding its earlier contributions in several theatres overseas, several aspects of its performance no longer suited our purpose. However, as I circulated round the trade stands at Farnborough I paused by that of Handley Page, my eye having been caught by the model of a new type of aircraft. While I was examining it a helpful representative approached and enquired if I was in need of information. "How high will it fly?" I asked. "We are not yet sure," came the reply. "Why do you wish to know?" And that was the beginning of a long and friendly relationship. The model on display was that of the Handley Page 'Dart Herald' transport aircraft, and this helped to set in motion a sequence of events that a small group of SAS Old Comrades still recall during their periodic reunions, now more than fifty years later.

Having discovered a potential aircraft, and with the existence of the 'SAS Skydivers', formed in 1961 after initial free fall parachute training courses designed to prepare the regiment for its new role in global warfare, I now decided to seek a suitable opportunity to carry out a team descent by not fewer than four parachutists from a height of approximately 30,000 feet, with a dual purpose. First, it was necessary to demonstrate that a team of highly trained free fallers could land loosely grouped within a selected target area, subject to adequate visibility, as a prelude to an operational task. Second, in the event of the trials proving successful, the facts should be put before higher authority, together with appropriate conclusions and recommendations. Although these aims remained in prospect, it became necessary partially to obscure them as the trials developed, both on account of security and in order to retain the interest of Handley Page, who, we believed, might be prepared to assist, particularly if the enterprise were to be coupled with the Dart Herald establishing a high altitude parachuting record. Such publicity, from which Handley Page would benefit, also made it possible to regard it as a sporting venture and the means of concealing a significant operational capability. This was still within the exploratory stage of parachuting for sport, the only previous participant in the United Kingdom being an individual who had unfortunately drowned when dropping intentionally into the sea while being filmed.

Before any definite decision could be made there was much research to be undertaken into the design and production of clothing and equipment suitable for use in temperatures likely to be lower than any to which isolated humans could previously have been exposed. As interest in this concept developed it became clear that we were about to become involved in a project of considerable complexity, with technical and scientific aspects for which we would require expert guidance. Fortunately, this was available and willingly provided by authoritative sources, including several imaginative and helpful scientists. It was also encouraging to observe the close interest that our pilot was taking in what had by then become a joint venture. Squadron Leader (retired) H.G. 'Hazel' Hazeldean, Chief Test Pilot of Handley Page, had every quality and expertise we could have wished for during our endeavours, and with his assistance we soon became familiar with all relevant features and characteristics of his aircraft. The manufacturers undertook to modify the Dart Herald for us, which included stripping the aircraft of all unnecessary equipment to reduce its weight and removing the port-side rear door to facilitate our exit. It was also necessary to set up an oxygen tube for each parachutist from the aircraft supply and a series of cabin notice lights that could be activated by the pilot on a pre-arranged system to notify the whole team of distances as we approached the drop-zone on Salisbury Plain.

Then came the joint discussion of the sequence of movements and actions by members of the team once airborne and the stages of preparation ahead of us. Some would be initiated by the pilot and others by me as leader of what had become an eight-man team. An early priority was a detailed discussion with Air Traffic Control at the Royal Aircraft Establishment at Farnborough, the staff of which could not have been more helpful. Their task was to assist the pilot during an approach to the drop-zone of sufficient distance to achieve the necessary climb from 10,000 to around 35,000 feet. The direction of the run-in to our exit point would depend on the prevailing wind, while the dropping point would have to be adjusted according to its strength. At an early stage of our preparations it became clear that because of military commitments the only period open for our trials was the second half of January 1962, and this limitation superimposed possible meteorological problems on an already complex project.

We were all in excellent physical shape, and every member of the team had undergone at least two sessions in a decompression chamber to minimise the risk of suffering from hypoxia. We had also experienced conditions of extreme low temperature in a cold room in order to test the efficiency of our clothing, knowing that hypothermia affects judgement and that any exposure of unprotected flesh would result in instant frostbite. In the last fifty years there have been significant advances in fabric design and manufacture, but the clothing with which we were provided was very traditional, the list including string vest, long woollen pants, woollen socks, heavy duty pullover, track suit, tank suit, windproof parachuting suit, silk inner gloves, leather outer gloves, balaclava helmet and arctic boots. We all made several jumps wearing oxygen masks and equipment, and as the day chosen for the jump approached we completed our series of rehearsal flights, which progressively familiarised the team of experienced parachutists, the aircraft flying at increasing altitudes of up to 32,000 feet. A practice jump was also made from the Dart Herald in order to check exit and slipstream characteristics, which vary between different types of aircraft. At this point we had the satisfaction of knowing that each stage of our preparation had gone according to plan, and I also sensed an air of quiet confidence, as well as determination to solve any problem we might not have foreseen or had underestimated. Just as important was the need to prevent enthusiasm from overriding judgement. It was going to be a test for each element involved: the aircraft, the pilots and the team of aerial pioneers.

It was on 30 January that our team's readiness coincided with the availability of the aircraft and suitable meteorological conditions of good visibility and acceptable ground wind level for what subsequently became known to those concerned as 'The High One'. The initial idea was to make two jumps in the day, the first from 25,000 feet and then another from the maximum altitude attainable by the aircraft. We took off from Boscombe Down, south-east of

Amesbury, and were approaching the drop-zone in the triangle between Tilshead, Chitterne and Shrewton when the pilot received a report that the cloud cover was too thick. By the time we had landed back at Boscombe Down the cloud cover had thinned, and after consultation with the Met Office there and discussion within the team it was agreed that it should be possible to make a jump before dusk. We took off again at around 1350 hours, our pilot determined to reach the maximum height possible in the prevailing conditions. The most noticeable aspect of the increase in altitude was the steady drop in air temperature as the climb continued. At 20,000 feet it was -30°C, and at -45°C the lowest limit of the aircraft's temperature gauge was reached. It took about half an hour to reach the drop-zone, but as the altitude was then only 31,500 and the rate of climb still over 200 feet per minute, Squadron Leader Hazeldean requested permission from Farnborough Radar to circle and make a further run in the course of ten to fifteen minutes. However, by then the head wind had increased to between 80 and 90 knots (approaching 100 mph) so it was another twenty minutes before the aircraft neared the drop-zone again. Five miles from the jumping point the Dart Herald had reached 33,700 feet, and the pilot of an observer aircraft in the vicinity reported the outside air temperature as in the vicinity of -55°C.

With two miles to go before we reached our planned exit point, we pulled the release cables of our individual 'bale out' oxygen bottles and disconnected our oxygen tubes from the main aircraft supply. Almost immediately one member, Lance Corporal Beaumont, slumped unconscious, suggesting a fault in his personal supply, and at the same moment the green exit light indicated the pilot's signal for us to jump. We reconnected Beaumont to the aircraft system, confident that he would soon recover, and although there had been a brief delay I gave the thumbs-up signal for the jump to go ahead. I went first, followed in quick succession by Staff Sergeant D. Hughes, Corporal B. Sanders, Corporal R. K. Norry, Corporal R. Reid, Lance Corporal T. Roberts and Sergeant P. Sherman. We jumped at 34,350 feet, and ahead of us was a free fall drop amounting to six miles before the need to activate our parachutes approximately three minutes later at 2,000 feet. Everyone was immediately struck by the intense cold, but the chief problem was the icing up of our goggles when the moisture from our eyeballs was transferred to the lenses. However, we were all able to see enough of our altimeters to gain an impression of the progress of our drop, falling at terminal velocity (over

230 mph at 34,000 feet, slowing to 120 mph at the moment of parachute deployment). Our ground party had lit a powerful flare in the middle of the drop-zone, and six of the seven of us who had jumped together landed loosely grouped within 300 yards of the flare.

There was an immediate feeling of immense achievement in setting a new team world record, but this elation was shattered when a farm worker hurried up with the news that he had seen one of us drop to the ground without his parachute. Corporal Keith Norry was an experienced parachutist with a record of over 160 free fall descents, and despite a detailed Board of Enquiry no explanation could subsequently be found to explain the cause of his failure to activate either his main or reserve parachute on this occasion, which predated the introduction of the automatic opening device. He was an immensely popular member of the regiment, and his funeral at Tidworth Military Cemetery is remembered by those who attended for the quite remarkable number of wreaths. Even now, fifty years later, the surviving members of those who parachuted with him reunite annually in order to keep in touch and lay another wreath on his grave.

Despite this sad fatality, the media were enthusiastic about the achievement, reflecting widespread interest in the technical as well as the personal aspects of our endeavour; but they did not report the happy outcome to the oxygen drama on the aircraft. Shortly after he had been reconnected to the aircraft supply, Peter Beaumont regained consciousness and, possibly reflecting his stamina as an outstanding cross country runner, struggled to his feet and lurched towards the exit. The pilots had been aware of what had happened and the second pilot made as if to go and help, but had to be restrained by his senior because he too would have severed his personal supply and become unconscious himself. So they could only watch Beaumont groggily make his belated exit, knowing that he would inevitably lose consciousness again. However, at some state in free fall his body responded to the increased oxygen level in the atmosphere and he became alert enough to activate his parachute at the correct height. Because of his delayed jump he landed a mile or two beyond the drop zone, but flagged down a passing baker's van and persuaded the driver to bring him to rejoin us, his usual composed and cheerful self but with little recall of the sequence of events.

Various military commitments then took priority, but we were able to enter our free fall team in the British National Parachute Championships, held at

Goodwood in April, where we managed to secure the top six places. This meant that as a team we were able to represent Great Britain in the Sixth World Parachute Championships in Orange, Massachusetts the following August, and it was there, as we were about to disperse, that Jacques Istel, a remarkable American of French extraction, invited me to take part in what he referred to as the Second World Para-Ski Race, due to take place in Vermont some months later. I was a bit non-committal, as it sounded an extremely hare-brained undertaking, but in the New Year he contacted me again and I agreed to travel to the aptly named Mad River Glen in early March. The race was open to teams of two, and a fit young American named Lewis 'Skip' Doolittle, on the staff of the Parachute Center at Orange, offered to be my partner.

On the day, a brisk wind was revealed by paper streamers dropped from the aircraft, a Noorduyn Norseman, to assist the teams in deciding when to jump. We were competing against the clock, and after the first jumper had left the aircraft there was then a maximum delay of five seconds between each of the following competitors. We were flying at about 2,500 feet above the mountain (5,800 feet above sea level), and on looking down the landscape appeared thick with trees. A parachute drop-zone had never previously been established at the top of a mountain, but here the orange cross showing our target was set in the famous Catamount Bowl. We knew that our skis had been taken up earlier by cable car and left to one side of the cross, so on landing we had to remove our parachutes, touch the centre of the red marker in the bowl, don our skis and set off on the trail that snaked through the forest down to the resort below, ending on a giant slalom course set up especially by the Mad River Glen personnel. I managed to land close to the target, while Skip avoided the trees but landed in a small ravine about 100 yards away. However, he quickly clambered back to the clearing and, being an accomplished skier, reached the finishing line just ahead of me. We were timed from the moment we left the aircraft until our skis crossed the line and were delighted to find that, because all the other competitors had had various problems, we were the winners. The event was one of the highlights of my parachuting experience, and the inscribed silver sugar bowl with which I was presented means as much to me as a championship medal.

Chapter 27

Eighty-Five Years of Shooting for Sport

Shooting is an amusement of a very rational nature, affording both pleasure and exercise: the pleasure, too, is of the most interesting kind, whilst the exercise which attends it administers, in a superior degree, to the health and vigour of the body, by expelling those gross humours which lurk within the human frame and frequently baffle the skill of the physician.

B. Thomas, *The Shooter's Guide* (1819)

Many of the preceding chapters have referred to sporting experiences with a shotgun, and it is understandable that the total of my shooting friends and acquaintances, in the course of these eighty-five years, has reached well into four figures. It is also natural that my sporting records should contain a liberal selection of activities undertaken with family and friends during most of these years, and it is not surprising that numerous contemporaries have retained memories of events and incidents that tally with my own.

The initial introduction to the use of a shotgun is very significant, and no aspect is of greater importance than safety. My father was particularly vigilant about this, and the aforementioned John Cowtan, close friend and Army contemporary, once told me of an experience comparable to one of my own. On a family shooting day, when he was six years old, he was armed with a stout stick and joined the beaters, until a drive came where, as a reward for his efforts, he was allowed to stand at one end of the line of guns as a spectator. Halfway through the drive a pheasant flew past him and he raised his stick in pretence of shooting it. Unfortunately, he allowed his stick to swing through the line of guns and was observed doing so by his father, who promptly ordered him to be escorted home and sent to bed for showing disregard for safety. Recounting this more than sixty years later, John said that at the time he cried bitterly at missing the rest of the day's sport, but that it was a lesson he never forgot. An experience of my own as a small boy was being sent home by my father after I had failed to secure behind me a field gate, thereby risking the potential escape of farm stock. Those days of such strict family discipline may now, I suspect, belong to the past, but what alternative means of stressing the need for permanent safety awareness might prove to be as effective?

My own serious interest in shooting began when I was given a .410 shotgun as a present on my eighth birthday. This was put to good use on rabbits, initially under supervision, in the fields surrounding my home, at times when they became a veritable plague, before myxomatosis swept the country in the mid-1950s. There are many ways of combining interest and enthusiasm with the vital awareness of the overriding importance of gun safety when introducing the younger generation to the essentials of the sport. By the time my two sons were shooting, a level of immunity to myxomatosis had built up, so the rabbit population had grown again, and the pursuit of them in the course of several holidays in Scotland gave the boys an excellent grounding in the sequence of procedures to be followed.

Early in our first stay as a family at what became a favourite location in Dumfriesshire we had been befriended by the local gamekeeper, Murray Martin, who, having satisfied himself that they were safe and competent shots, was more than happy to have the boys help him in his battle to control the local infestation of rabbits. We would assemble at dusk, which in July meant late in the evening, at the gamekeeper's cottage. He had modified the back of his 4 x 4 pick-up to accommodate a bench seat fixed in the centre of the open body, so that guns could shoot from either side of the vehicle. Shooting commenced some time after 10.00 pm and thereafter continued unabated, assisted by a powerful hand-operated lamp. The rabbits were so plentiful that several would be shot in one area before the 28 bore shotguns the boys were using were unloaded and put down to allow one or both boys to jump down and collect the carcases. We would then move on to another area where the guns would be reloaded and a whole lot more rabbits dealt with. By this means the total number of rabbits shot before midnight usually exceeded a hundred, and the experience, repeated several times in the fortnight's holiday, was among the highlights of our stay. As a matter of routine, the unloading of a shotgun every time it was laid down became automatic and contributed to the boys' awareness of the ever-present need for safety as the primary consideration during all forms of shooting. It may have been partly as a result of the reputation they gained of being thoroughly reliable shots that they received an invitation one year, through the generosity of the Tylden-Wright family, to join a shooting party on a moor in Inverness-shire, where each was able to bag his first grouse on the Glorious Twelfth.

One of the advantages of shooting informally at home with family and friends is the flexibility that can be part of country life. When I had sporadic periods of leave from active service, my father would sometimes arrange a day, or even just a few hours, of rough shooting for my benefit and occasionally that of my brother Peter, who was commissioned from Dartmouth into the Royal Navy in 1940. The occasions during the war when we were at home at the same time were very few, so it was a memorable day when Peter's and my own home leave coincided during a shooting season and the three of us managed to shoot together.

In 1949, after my father's retirement, my parents decided to move from our North Country home to enjoy the milder climate and the field sports in the South West, having found a small sporting estate on the edge of Exmoor, several miles north of Dulverton. Notwithstanding my love of Northumberland and proud membership of its county regiment, I had little option, as a bachelor at the time, other than to regard their home as my base when military duties permitted. However, there were definite attractions where field sports were concerned, which helped to counterbalance the loss of grouse shooting and wildfowling within easy reach to which I had become accustomed. My regimental links with Northumberland were unaffected, so I was able to keep in regular contact with that county, and the closer I became associated with Exmoor and its environment the more I appreciated its field sports and friendly natives.

In the early 1950s my father also bought a stretch of fishing on the River Exe, including part of the Little Exe above its confluence with the Barle, together with thirty acres of adjoining land, from Mrs Cecilia Kynaston, the owner of Burston Farm in the neighbouring parish of Morebath. Her son Nicolas, who became a world-renowned cathedral and concert organist, learnt to play the organ in the parish church in the days before electricity was connected to the building, and the instrument had to be hand-pumped by his brother. Some four acres of one of the river meadows were marsh and scrubby woodland, and here my father and I created a nature reserve, with a pond of nearly an acre containing an island to provide a safe area for ground-nesting birds. For a number of years in the 1960s and early 1970s Jack and Beryl Hulbert, a pair of ecologist civil servants, used to come from London for a long weekend, pitching a tent and setting up mist nets to enable them to catch and ring a remarkable number of species.

By the early 1960s Burston Farm had been sold to a Polish family, who had settled in the West Country through their connection with Auberon Herbert, the owner of nearby Pixton Park. He had served with Polish forces during the war, his flat feet having precluded him from the British Army. My father and I regularly shot pheasants with Auberon, and it was through him that my father was given an introduction to the Sohanick family of Burston Farm, who gave him permission to go rough shooting over their land whenever he wished. So while I was on leave and staying with my parents, I accompanied my father on several forays over these fields, most of which were north-facing and rose to a level from which we could look across the valley towards an isolated thatched farmhouse nestling near the top of its own wooded combe. On one such day I happened to remark light-heartedly to my father that it looked just the sort of place I would like to retire to when I left the Army; but I then dismissed this as a fanciful idea and put it out of my mind. However, some time later, my father wrote to tell me he had heard locally that the property might be coming up for sale. At the time I was serving in Germany, but I took an early opportunity to return to England in order to take a closer look at this place that had caught my eye several years earlier. I knew it was set apart from the small hamlet situated half a mile away on lower ground, but I had not realised that its approach lane had become so broken up and strewn with boulders that it was accessible only by foot or on horseback.

As I walked up the steep track I passed the remains of six derelict cars that had broken down in the attempt to traverse it and had then been abandoned. However, when I finally reached the house, although I found it in a state of extreme dilapidation, with its ancient thatched roof decorative rather than effective, the setting was so idyllic that I persuaded myself to look at its problems with an open mind. This turned out to be the right approach, although the necessary renovation turned out to be considerably more dramatic than I had visualised. As I was still posted in Germany, I engaged an architect to oversee the work. He advised replacing the thatch with tiles, but when the thatch was removed it was discovered that the rafters were rotten, and when the rafters were removed most of the walls fell in. However, nearly fifty years ago, after eighteen months' work, it became my home, where I was joined a few years later by my wife and, in due course, our sons.

My isolated farmhouse came with some sixty acres of pasture and woodland that at first became just an extension of the rough shooting we already enjoyed over Burston Farm to the south. While I was still a bachelor my parents moved from their home, which had become larger than they needed, into my house as caretakers, and my own shooting was confined to the rare occasions when I was on leave from distant parts. However, in 1971 Burston Farm again came on the market. My father and I decided to buy it jointly, and we were fortunate to find an excellent bailiff in Cecil Crudge, who farmed it for us together with the acres at Combeland. This almost coincided with my retirement from the Army, and although I then returned to Cambridge to complete my academic studies that had been interrupted by the outbreak of the Second World War thirty-two years earlier, I was able to devote a certain amount of time to developing a shoot. With the acquisition of Burston it became possible to erect a release pen for pheasants in one of the woods there and to put another one in a small wood at Combeland. For several seasons I bought in a few hundred day-old chicks from a local game farm and raised them in temporary shelters erected in the field behind my house.

At this stage my knowledge and experience of pheasant rearing and management was limited to observation and keen interest from boyhood onwards, but I still had much to learn, some of it the hard way, although I did engage a part-time keeper to help when I had to be in Cambridge. One year there was a violent thunderstorm in the middle of the night when the chicks were only a few days old, and the deluge was such that their shelters became flooded. In the course of several hours my wife and I managed to rescue the majority by lamplight from impending disaster, but her subsequent pointed comments probably led to an early decision to buy six-week-old poults in the future, which were put straight into the release pens in the woods. At this stage I was able to gather a group of keen shooting friends together, including Stewart Woodman, who had been an Army Aviation pilot before studying medicine and becoming one of our local doctors. We shot six or seven times between the beginning of November and the end of January and were very satisfied if we achieved bags of fifty or sixty pheasants.

Once the shoot had become organised for driven game it became an annual pleasure to issue invitations to various friends for one of the days. There was a regular team of beaters, initially local farming men who were free to join in on a Saturday, together with Fred Collins, one of the Exmoor National Park wardens; but latterly the beaters have come mainly from two families, the Pincombes and Stonemans. The three Stoneman daughters joined in progressively as they became old enough, always remained cheerful even on the cold, wet days, and eventually brought their younger brother, who started when he could only just last out the day, but never flagged and was as good as a spaniel at diving into overgrown patches of brambles. The other two regular beaters are the brothers Leslie and Geoffrey Payne from Morebath, Leslie having been a stalwart almost from the beginning, bicycling from the village as a boy and now completing over forty years with us. The friends who came to shoot over the years either lived in the West Country or were happy to travel from further afield. My brother Peter came from his home in Hampshire, and Tom Rylands, a second cousin, still travels down from Cheshire. His mother Denise was a most talented artist and painted a lovely picture of the shoot in November 1982, featuring all the family as well as the guns. It depicted a particular annual event, known as the Regimental Day, when erstwhile Fifth Fusiliers assembled. For several years Algy Parsons came from further west in Devon, and one year John Oakley made the journey down from Shrewsbury, but for a decade or more the core of the team comprised David Colbeck, Robert Ferguson and Robbie Leith-Macgregor, who became known as the 'Three Musketeers'. Robbie and his wife Pam from London, with Robert and his wife Eve from Manningford Bruce, would descend on David and his wife Andrée near Exeter for the weekend and spend the Saturday shooting with us, the wives joining in for lunch and the afternoon. Latterly, David's son Simon, also a Fifth Fusilier, was able to come from Gloucestershire.

For many years the Fusiliers were joined by Anthony Barrowclough, former Ombudsman, and a regular addition to the Regimental Day was

Stewart Woodman, who also featured on another memorable occasion. It so happened that during 1987 I had attended several military events and met friends of long standing with whom I had served at intervals through my career. In conversation it somehow emerged that all of them were still keen shooting men, and I came up with the idea of inviting them all on the same day the following season. This proved to be very acceptable to Roly Gibbs, Bala Bredin, Peter Cavendish, Tony Deane-Drummond, Jack Dye and Tony Jeapes, and developed into a splendid weekend, with the shooting on Saturday followed by a dinner for the guns and their wives that Sarah and I hosted at the Carnarvon Arms Hotel in the neighbouring village. John Cowtan and his wife Rose were unable to come, but we remedied that omission later in the season. Through the years I had always tried to have my camera with me, and after dinner I put on a slide show featuring pictures of all the participants in the different parts of the world we had served, including Palestine, Kenya and Aden. As you can imagine, this stimulated many memories, and as the evening drew on the problem was trying to stem the flow of reminiscences.

Our boys at that time attended the wonderful small primary school at Cutcombe, on the edge of Exmoor, where the practice was to sit the children down after morning assembly on a Monday and encourage them to talk about what they had been doing over the weekend. The school being where it was, farming and field sports often featured, and a day's hunting was regularly described in detail. On this occasion we learnt that Alexander had been enthusiastic about the pheasant shooting at Combeland, when they had "all been soldier friends of Daddy's. One was a Field Marshal and all the others were Generals, except Dr Woodman." Peter, then aged 5½, had obviously thought this sounded a little disparaging so immediately chipped in with the remark that "anybody can be a soldier, but you have to be clever to be a doctor." As the school was in Stewart Woodman's practice area this inevitably got back to him, and he was delighted to have received such a warm endorsement.

Another event that was a regular for several years was the Boys' Day, when prep-school friends of our boys were invited, with their fathers to act as safety officers. The day grew from a clay pigeon shooting competition we had organised one summer holidays at the Shooting School run the other side of our parish by the inimitable Rod Brammer. Having seen the standard of most of the boys participating, I knew they would enjoy being tested by real pheasants, and this was indeed the case. The day proved immensely popular each year in the Christmas holidays, despite the fact that the tradition of good weather on Combeland shoot days was broken on several occasions, once with regular showers of drenching rain and once when the temperature dropped during the day and a light drizzle falling on frozen ground caused all the fathers some consternation as they had to negotiate their vehicles down our steep drive, which had become something of a skating rink. Inevitably, the shoot was discontinued when the boys dispersed to different senior schools with other calls on their time, but it is a delight now to have our own sons home regularly from their respective occupations.

Since the early days of the shoot my wife has assisted in a variety of ways, including the complexities of juggling being in the kitchen to cook lunch, acting as a stop on several drives and producing refreshments in the middle of the morning, a particularly popular feature on cold days. There was also the introduction and participation of our two sons as they became familiar with the traditional progress of shoot organisation, not overlooking the problems that may arise. However, in retrospect, our days usually went very smoothly, as loose ends were dealt with and all the necessary arrangements fell into place. Latterly, I have been able to hand over much of the routine running of the shoot to Alexander, ably assisted by Peter, leaving me with the option of deciding when to participate and for how long on any particular day. I have also discovered how much satisfaction may be had in handling one's dogs, when no longer fully involved in the detailed management of the day's programme. We now have Dixie, the latest addition to what, back in the 1960s, my free fall team members used to refer to as my 'black ladies'. She is the twelfth black Labrador I have had since the incomparable Dinah, just as beautiful as all her predecessors and already giving the impression of being just as much of a character.

As time passes, one of the many pleasures related to shooting later in life lies in the scrutiny of old records, and particularly those of one's own family. My personal preference is for my father's game book covering his last thirty years, until he finally gave up shooting at the age of 90. Much of what I learned about game shooting came from him, and that, I believe, is how sporting traditions persisted within many of the shooting families I have known. In the meantime, my own participation continues beyond the stage I could reasonably have foreseen, and I am delighted, at the age of 93, to have had my shotgun licence renewed for a further five years; it will be kept safely, together with my annual fishing licence. And, of course, I have the store of wonderful memories of eighty-five years of shooting and fishing in a wide variety of settings, sometimes alone, other times with family or friends, and more often than not with the companionship of my Labrador.

'Long may ye live – my much respected patrons – to love your Queen, to adorn your country, and to enjoy British field sports.'

From *The Modern Shooter* by Captain Lacy, published 1842

Appendix

The General's Black Labradors

Dinah	1936–1949
Duchess	1945–1958
Diamond	1953–1966
Dawn	1959–1970
Dimple	1965–1971
Dora	1971–1985
Dimpsey	1977–1992
Dinnet	1984–1998
Dee	1988–2002
Dorrie	1995–2005
Diri	2001–
Dixie	2012–